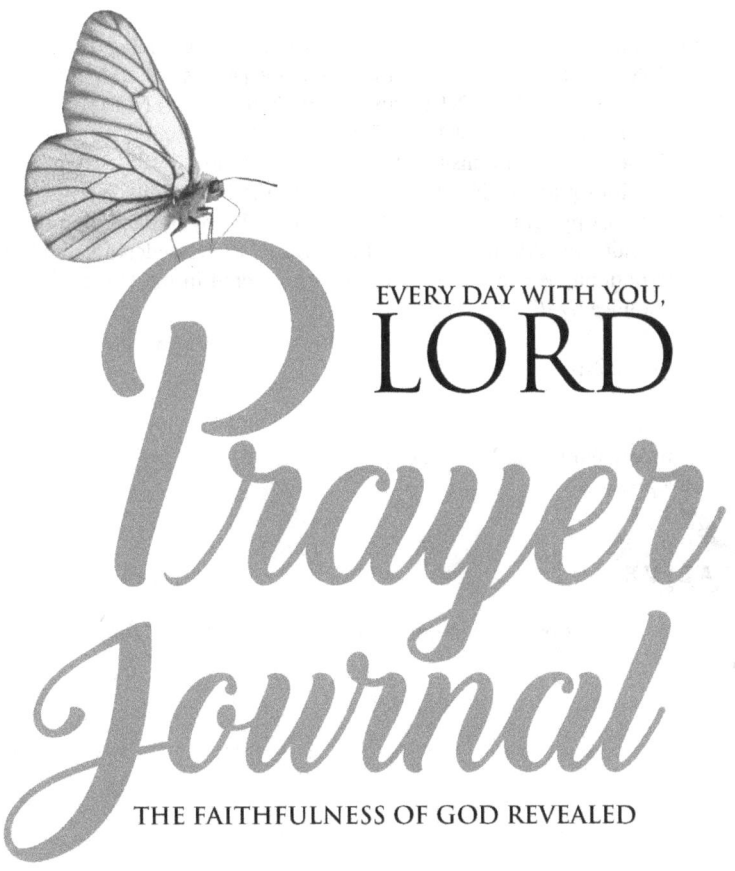

EVERY DAY WITH YOU,
LORD
Prayer Journal
THE FAITHFULNESS OF GOD REVEALED

KELLY SIMMONS

EVERY DAY WITH YOU, LORD: PRAYER JOURNAL
Copyright © 2024 by Kelly Simmons

All rights reserved. Neither this publication nor any part of this publication may be reproduced or transmitted in any form or by any means, electronic or mechanical, including photocopying, recording or any information storage and retrieval system, without permission in writing from the author.

Scripture quotations marked (NKJV) are taken from the New King James Version®. Copyright © 1982 by Thomas Nelson, Inc. Used by permission. All rights reserved. • Scripture quotations marked (NLT) are taken from the Holy Bible, New Living Translation, copyright ©1996, 2004, 2015 by Tyndale House Foundation. Used by permission of Tyndale House Publishers, Carol Stream, Illinois 60188. All rights reserved. • Scripture quotations marked (NIV) are taken from the Holy Bible, New International Version®, NIV®. Copyright © 1973, 1978, 1984, 2011 by Biblica, Inc.™ Used by permission of Zondervan. All rights reserved worldwide. www.zondervan.comThe "NIV" and "New International Version" are trademarks registered in the United States Patent and Trademark Office by Biblica, Inc.™

ISBN: 978-1-4866-2581-9

Word Alive Press
119 De Baets Street Winnipeg, MB R2J 3R9
www.wordalivepress.ca

Cataloguing in Publication information can be obtained from Library and Archives Canada.

This Journal Belongs to:

_____

*When You said, "Seek My face,"
My heart said to You, "Your face, LORD, I will seek."*

Psalm 27:8 (NKJV)

ACKNOWLEDGEMENTS

The very first attribute of God I came to know after giving my life to Him was His faithfulness. From the very beginning, He showed me that He is dependable, capable, willing, and able to take care of me, protect me, and provide for me. He showed Himself to be everything I will ever need, and in doing so, revealed Himself to be faithful.

Thank You, Father God, for Your awesome loving kindness towards me. Thank You for allowing me to write this book to provide a place for others to come to know You as a faithful loving Father as they fill each page with Your personal word to them and answers to prayer. Thank You for Your unfailing love for me, and the privilege to be given this work to write. To God be the glory, great things He has done!

"Therefore know that the LORD your God, He is God, the faithful God who keeps covenant and mercy for a thousand generations with those who love Him and keep His commandments;"

Deuteronomy 7:9 (NKJV)

How To Use This Journal

Welcome to *Every Day with You, Lord – The Faithfulness of God Revealed*. Whether you're a brand-new Christian or have been walking with the Lord from your youth, we all go through a process and stages of learning about the character and faithfulness of our God and Father. Even after walking with Him for years, there is always yet another aspect of His awesome ability, love and power that is fresh and new to us. Really, the key to understanding faithfulness as it pertains to God is wrapped up in one little word: trust. Trusting and believing that God will do what He has promised. Whether or not we are willing to admit it to ourselves, we have all had times in our lives when we have questioned whether God will answer our prayer, meet our need, or make provision for some required necessity, leading us to two seemingly *big* words: what if? What if God *doesn't* come through for me? What will happen then? What we're really asking ourselves is, what if God doesn't keep His promise? It looks bad in print, but if we are honest most of us have pondered similar questions at one time or another during our walk with Him.

This prayer journal was created to help us answer that question once and for all. It will lead us through a very special, and deeply personal year of prayer and devotional times with the Lord, leading us to the answers we need to forever silence all doubts. It will take us on a journey to the revelation of the everlasting faithfulness of our God. It's arranged in such a way to aid us on our journey to understanding the multifaceted depth of God's character, loving kindness, tender mercies, and yes, *faithfulness*!

There are several specific areas provided in which to make journal entries. Making consistent entries is the key. At the end of the year, you too, as did Sarah, Abraham, Jacob, David, and countless others, will come to know and settle in your heart, that He is truly faithful who promised (Hebrews 11:11).

TRUST

reliance on the integrity, strength or ability of a person or thing;
confident expectation of something; hope;
one upon which a person relies.[1]

---

[1] *Webster's Universal College Dictionary* (2001), s.v. "trust."

Categories for Journaling

The first area provided for entries is entitled *This Week's Prayer List*. Here you will find a place to make requests on behalf of others. This is an important aspect of your prayer journaling journey, as we are admonished within Scripture to pray for the needs of others (1 Timothy 2:1). As we do, two things can happen within our own lives. First, we fulfill the mandate given to us from the Lord, and in so doing, also reap the rewards of obedience to it. Jesus tells us that whatever we do for another person in need, we have done as if it had been done for Him directly (Matthew 25:40). Remember too, the principle of sowing and reaping. You always reap *more* than you sow. Sowing seeds of offered prayer on behalf of another can yield returns of bountiful harvest in similar likeness to a monetary seed that's been sown.

Now is a good time to encourage you when thinking of those whom you might add to your prayer list, to include the names of those who may have hurt you or have brought problems or pain into your life. Yes, we need to pray for our enemies, and those who are not enemies at all, but who have acted in ways that reflect the *behavior* of an enemy. We are told in Matthew 5:44 to pray for those who despitefully use you and persecute you. Although this is not always an easy task, we do well to obey the Lord's command. In praying for our enemies, we place ourselves in a posture to release all bitterness, resentment, and unforgiveness, all of which can hinder us from receiving answers to our own prayers.

So as difficult as it may seem, add them to your prayer list. Ask the Lord for the grace to pray for and forgive them, keeping the door open to receive all that God has for you. In giving the gift of forgiveness, we sow the seeds of love and obedience, and position ourselves to reap the harvest of an open heaven.

The second benefit of praying for the needs of others comes as we receive praise reports about those for whom we have prayed. In witnessing the faithfulness of God in the lives of others, our own faith will increase and begin to grow. We can know that what God has done for another, He will also do for us. It really is a two-fold blessing.

The second area to make entries is entitled *My Personal Prayer Requests*. This is the area which you are encouraged to use to seek the Lord for the things you need personally. Whether it be prayer for direction, physical or emotional healing, or something else, this is where you need to make it personal, and open yourself up before the Lord with your whole heart. John 16:24 tells us to ask the Lord, and we shall receive. If we ask, we will find that God is faithful to answer, and to show Himself mighty on our behalf. Truly He is *El Shaddai*, the God who is more than enough, and *Jehovah Jireh*, the God who provides. There is no need to be shy; ask big things of our great big God.

You will also find a place provided to include Scripture references related to the needs for which you are praying (more on this later). This is an important step.

When we pray in accordance with the Word of God, we can be assured that we will receive that for which we ask. This of course means that we must *know* what Scripture has to say.

We must spend time reading the Word of God on a regular basis. Spending time in the Word of God is the most crucial part of getting to know our God and Father. This is where He speaks to our hearts, gives instruction, ministers to what ails us, brings correction, and transforms us by the renewing of our minds. This is where our relationship with Him really grows. When we take time to read the Scriptures, we are taking time to get to know Him, and to understand His heart.

A prayer journal, or any other means of drawing near to God without also adding the Word of God, is not enough. Communication is a two-way street. We can hear God speak at any time of the day or night by simply opening the pages of Scripture. There are answers for every issue of life contained within its pages. All we need to do to partake of its rich rewards and wisdom, is prayerfully open its pages and open our heart to receive from God. The Word of God is alive and will always impart new life, which leads us to the third area provided, entitled, *Quiet Moments Daily Devotional Time.*

In this area you will find provision for entries made for personal words spoken to you from the Lord directly, as you spend daily quiet time with Him in prayer and meditation in the Word of God. You may receive new or clearer revelation of Scripture, direction, or personal instruction during your time of fellowship with Him. This is the place to record whatever you have received from Him during those times.

The section titled *A Light for My Path*, is where you may incorporate sermon notes taken from the Word of God spoken from the pulpit, during Sunday morning church services.

It's truly amazing how God can speak a direct word to each of His children personally, through the gift of the preached Word. We serve an on time, personal, and dedicated God and Father, who is deeply committed to our individual growth and success. Praise be to God who always causes us to triumph! (2 Corinthians 2:14).

Now comes the entry made at the end of each week entitled, *Praise Reports - The Week in Review*. This is where you may input anything at all that the Lord has done for you over the past week, or any prayer answered for either yourself or of someone for whom you have prayed. This brings us to the final entry heading, *Song of Gratitude.*

This is the place to express and put into writing your admiration and praise to the Lord for His unfailing loving-kindness, and attentive answers to prayer throughout the year. What a wonderful way to conclude a year of beautiful fellowship with the Lord and to show our appreciation for His faithfulness toward us.

Although beginning a new year in this way is nice, it isn't necessary to begin your journey on the first of January. Any day is a good day to start your journaling journey. Just stick with it for the duration of one full year. Your part is to consistently make each entry, God will do the rest.

At the end of the year, you will have tasted and seen that the Lord, He is good! (Psalm 34:8) Afterward, whatever the calendar date, you will be filled with new hope and joyful expectation, knowing with unwavering assurance, that the Lord is God, and His faithfulness endures forever!

Who to Remember in Prayer

Every time I think of you, I give thanks to my God. Whenever I pray, I make my requests for all of you with joy,

Philippians 1:3–4 (NLT)

- Husband
- Children, Adult Children & Their Spouses, Grandchildren, Family
- Pastors
- Church Family & Friends
- Government / Leadership / Employers
- Enemies

Ever since I first heard of your strong faith in the Lord Jesus and your love for God's people everywhere, I have not stopped thanking God for you. I pray for you constantly, asking God, the glorious Father of our Lord Jesus Christ, to give you spiritual wisdom and insight so that you might grow in your knowledge of God. I pray that your hearts will be flooded with light so that you can understand the confident hope he has given to those he called—his holy people who are his rich and glorious inheritance.

Ephesians 1:15–18 (NLT)

What Should I Pray For?

In this manner, therefore, pray: Our Father in heaven, Hallowed be Your name. Your kingdom come. Your will be done on earth, as it is in heaven. Give us this day our daily bread. And forgive us our debts, as we forgive our debtors. And do not lead us into temptation, But deliver us from the evil one. For Yours is the kingdom and the power and the glory forever. Amen.

Matthew 6:9–13 (NKJV)

In this familiar passage of Scripture, Jesus Himself gives us the model for prayer. The instruction, however, is not only to *repeat* the verses, but instead, it has been given to us as an outline to aid us in knowing what things we ought to address in prayer. What better example to draw from for direction in prayer than the one provided by the Lord Himself? Let's summarize the outline:

- The Will of God for our Lives
- Daily Needs & Concerns (*Spiritual and Physical)
- Confession of Sin
- Extending Forgiveness
- Guidance, Direction and Protection

Jesus begins by telling us what request should top our prayer list, saying, "Your Kingdom come. Your will be done." The will of God for our lives is our starting point. Truth be told, most often it's not the will of the Father that tops our requests, but our own will. Not His desire, but our desire. Not His wants, but ours. Not His plan, but our plan. Thank you Lord for Your intervention, wisdom, and concern for the fruitfulness and effectiveness of our prayer life!

He shows us the correct method in which to pray in order that we may, as promised, have the things that we ask for, that the Father may be glorified, and that our joy be made full (John 14:13–14; 16:24).

This, then, is the crux of it. First comes our excitement at the possibility of answered prayer, followed by deflated hopes as we learn that those prayers must be in alignment with what God wants instead of what we want. A heart with deflated hopes should not be the case, nor does it have to be. It is like the lie that was whispered to Eve so long ago in the garden. But it is still used on us today. Why? Because it worked back then and is still bringing deception even now. But praise be to God, it doesn't have to work any longer! The serpent made Eve think that God was holding out on her, keeping her from what was best in life. God had given her everything that she could ever want or hope for, and desired to keep her *from* a life of troubles and pain. Does God really want what's best for you? or is He really keeping you from having the good things in life? This was the question, wrapped in doubt and deception, that was whispered to Eve that fateful day in the garden. In hindsight, we all know the answer, but the enemy speaks the same lie to us today, asking, If you can only have what *God* wants, will you really get what *you* want? The answer is the same for us as it was for Eve, yes!

Don't consider the lies of the enemy any longer. Don't let your prayers be hindered by doubts of *what if?* Whose report are we going to believe? Confidently align your prayers with the will of the Father and watch what happens. You will find, as did the Apostle Paul, that God will do exceedingly abundantly *above* all that we ask for, or even has entered our mind! (Ephesians 3:20)

Personalizing the Word in Prayer

In the pages where your personal prayer requests are recorded, you will find a section to include a Scripture reference for the request that's being made. For instance, if you are praying for healing for yourself or a loved one, you may select a verse that pertains to healing found within Scripture, such as Isaiah 53:5, *By His stripes we are healed*, and pray in alignment with it.

God spoke the entire world into existence with the power and authority of His spoken Word (Genesis 1:3). When a believer prays in faith, by the authority of the name of Jesus, the results can be powerful (James 5:16). God has given each one of His children the authority to use both His name and His Word for the things we have need of on the earth. When we pray God's Word, we are in essence saying, Thy will be done Lord—Your Word and Your will be made manifest in my life—here on earth as it is in heaven. In praying the Word of God, we can personalize the promises of God found in His Word and apply them to our lives. We make the promises personal to us by taking ownership of them and receiving them by faith, as if they have already been done for us. (Mark 11:23–24) Put your name in it. Say, "It's mine, I'll take it! Thank You Jesus!" We're extending our faith believing that what God promised, He is also able to perform (Romans 4:21).

There's a saying that a dear and wonderful pastor I knew used to repeat regularly to the congregation: "God said it. I believe it, and that settles it!"

What He says, He will do! Don't allow the seed of your faith to wither in the waiting. It's by faith *and* patience that we inherit the promises of God (Hebrews 6:11–12). So have faith, mix it with patience, and look up with expectancy. He who promised is faithful.

My Personal Prayer Requests
Week Twenty-One

Delight yourself also in the Lord, and He shall give you the desires of your heart. Commit your way to the Lord, trust also in Him, and He shall bring it to pass.

Psalm 37:4–5 (NKJV)

EXAMPLE

Date: _August 18, 2024_

Prayer Request:

Lord, I'm in need of new school clothes for my three children. I have been laid off from work for 3 months now and they start school in two weeks' time. They are also in need of new school supplies. Please send provision for these needs, Lord, and I thank You for them. In Jesus name, AMEN

Scripture Promise:

And my God shall supply all your need according to His riches in glory by Christ Jesus. Phil. 4:19 (NKJV)

Date Answered: _____

This Week's Prayer List
Week One

I urge you, first of all, to pray for all people. Ask God to help them; intercede on their behalf, and give thanks for them.

1 Timothy 2:1 (NLT)

Name: _____

Date: _____

Prayer Request:

_____
_____
_____
_____

Name: _____

Date: _____

Prayer Request:

_____
_____
_____
_____

My Personal Prayer Requests

Delight yourself also in the Lord, and He shall give you the desires of your heart. Commit your way to the Lord, trust also in Him, and He shall bring it to pass.

Psalm 37:4–5 (NKJV)

Date: _____

Prayer Request:

_____
_____
_____
_____
_____
_____
_____

Scripture Promise:

_____
_____
_____

Quiet Moments with You
Daily Devotions

WEEK ONE

Then the Lord came and stood and called as at other times, "Samuel! Samuel!" And Samuel answered, "Speak, for Your servant hears."

1 Samuel 3:10 (NKJV)

MONDAY:

Date:

TUESDAY:

Date:

WEDNESDAY:

Date:

Speak to My Heart, Lord

THURSDAY:

Date:

FRIDAY:

Date:

SATURDAY:

Date:

Sunday Service
A Light for My Path

WEEK ONE

*I was glad when they said to me,
"Let us go into the house of the Lord."*

Psalm 122:1 (NKJV)

Date: _____ Speaker: _____

Sermon Title: _____

Scripture Text: _____

Notes:

_____
_____
_____
_____
_____
_____
_____
_____
_____
_____
_____

Praise Reports

The Week in Review

WEEK ONE

Come and see what our God has done,
what awesome miracles he performs for people!

Psalm 66:5 (NLT)

This Week's Prayer List
Week Two

I urge you, first of all, to pray for all people. Ask God to help them; intercede on their behalf, and give thanks for them.

1 Timothy 2:1 (NLT)

Name: _____

Date: _____

Prayer Request:
_____
_____
_____
_____

Name: _____

Date: _____

Prayer Request:
_____
_____
_____
_____

My Personal Prayer Requests

Delight yourself also in the Lord, and He shall give you the desires of your heart. Commit your way to the Lord, trust also in Him, and He shall bring it to pass.

Psalm 37:4–5 (NKJV)

Date: _____

Prayer Request:

_____
_____
_____
_____
_____
_____
_____
_____

Scripture Promise:

_____
_____
_____

Quiet Moments with You
Daily Devotions

WEEK TWO

Then the Lord came and stood and called as at other times, "Samuel! Samuel!" And Samuel answered, "Speak, for Your servant hears."

1 Samuel 3:10 (NKJV)

MONDAY:

Date:

___
___
___
___
___
___
___
___
___
___
___
___
___
___
___
___
___

TUESDAY:

Date:

WEDNESDAY:

Date:

Speak to My Heart, Lord

THURSDAY:

Date:

FRIDAY:

Date:

SATURDAY:

Date:

Sunday Service
A Light for My Path

WEEK TWO

I was glad when they said to me,
"Let us go into the house of the Lord."

Psalm 122:1 (**NKJV**)

Date: _____ Speaker: _____

Sermon Title: _____

Scripture Text: _____

Notes:

_____
_____
_____
_____
_____
_____
_____
_____
_____
_____
_____
_____

Praise Reports

The Week in Review

WEEK TWO

*Come and see what our God has done,
what awesome miracles he performs for people!*

Psalm 66:5 (**NLT**)

WEEK THREE

THIS WEEK'S PRAYER LIST
Week Three

I urge you, first of all, to pray for all people. Ask God to help them; intercede on their behalf, and give thanks for them.

1 Timothy 2:1 (NLT)

Name: _____

Date: _____

Prayer Request:

_____
_____
_____
_____

Name: _____

Date: _____

Prayer Request:

_____
_____
_____
_____

My Personal Prayer Requests
Week Three

Delight yourself also in the Lord, and He shall give you the desires of your heart. Commit your way to the Lord, trust also in Him, and He shall bring it to pass.

Psalm 37:4–5 (**NKJV**)

Date: _____

Prayer Request:

_____
_____
_____
_____
_____
_____
_____
_____
_____

Scripture Promise:

_____
_____
_____

Quiet Moments with You
Daily Devotions

WEEK THREE

Then the Lord came and stood and called as at other times, "Samuel! Samuel!" And Samuel answered, "Speak, for Your servant hears."

1 Samuel 3:10 (**NKJV**)

MONDAY:

Date:

TUESDAY:

Date:

_____
_____
_____
_____
_____
_____

WEDNESDAY:

Date:

_____
_____
_____
_____
_____
_____
_____

Speak to My Heart, Lord

THURSDAY:

Date:

FRIDAY:

Date:

SATURDAY:

Date:

Sunday Service
A Light for My Path

WEEK THREE

I was glad when they said to me,
"Let us go into the house of the Lord."

Psalm 122:1 (**NKJV**)

Date: _____ Speaker: _____

Sermon Title: _____

Scripture Text: _____

Notes:

_____
_____
_____
_____
_____
_____
_____
_____
_____
_____
_____
_____

Praise Reports

The Week in Review

WEEK THREE

Come and see what our God has done,
what awesome miracles he performs for people!

Psalm 66:5 (NLT)

This Week's Prayer List
Week Four

I urge you, first of all, to pray for all people. Ask God to help them; intercede on their behalf, and give thanks for them.

1 Timothy 2:1 (NLT)

Name: _____

Date: _____

Prayer Request:

_____
_____
_____
_____

Name: _____

Date: _____

Prayer Request:

_____
_____
_____
_____

My Personal Prayer Requests
Week Four

Delight yourself also in the Lord, and He shall give you the desires of your heart. Commit your way to the Lord, trust also in Him, and He shall bring it to pass.

Psalm 37:4–5 (NKJV)

Date: _____

Prayer Request:

_____
_____
_____
_____
_____
_____
_____
_____
_____

Scripture Promise:

_____
_____
_____

Quiet Moments with You
Daily Devotions

WEEK FOUR

Then the Lord came and stood and called as at other times, "Samuel! Samuel!" And Samuel answered, "Speak, for Your servant hears."

1 Samuel 3:10 (**NKJV**)

MONDAY:

Date:

___
___
___
___
___
___
___
___
___
___
___
___

TUESDAY:

Date:

WEDNESDAY:

Date:

Speak to My Heart, Lord

THURSDAY:

Date:

FRIDAY:

Date:

SATURDAY:

Date:

Sunday Service
A Light for My Path

WEEK FOUR

I was glad when they said to me,
"Let us go into the house of the Lord."

Psalm 122:1 (NKJV)

Date: _____ Speaker: _____

Sermon Title: _____

Scripture Text: _____

Notes:

_____
_____
_____
_____
_____
_____
_____
_____
_____
_____

Praise Reports

The Week in Review

WEEK FOUR

*Come and see what our God has done,
what awesome miracles he performs for people!*

Psalm 66:5 (NLT)

This Week's Prayer List

Week Five

I urge you, first of all, to pray for all people. Ask God to help them; intercede on their behalf, and give thanks for them.

1 Timothy 2:1 (NLT)

Name: _____

Date: _____

Prayer Request:
_____
_____
_____
_____

Name: _____

Date: _____

Prayer Request:
_____
_____
_____
_____

My Personal Prayer Requests
Week Five

Delight yourself also in the Lord, and He shall give you the desires of your heart. Commit your way to the Lord, trust also in Him, and He shall bring it to pass.

Psalm 37:4–5 (**NKJV**)

Date: _____

Prayer Request:

_____
_____
_____
_____
_____
_____
_____
_____
_____

Scripture Promise:

_____
_____
_____

Quiet Moments with You
Daily Devotions

WEEK FIVE

Then the Lord came and stood and called as at other times,
"Samuel! Samuel!" And Samuel answered,
"Speak, for Your servant hears."

1 Samuel 3:10 (NKJV)

MONDAY:

Date:

TUESDAY:

Date:

WEDNESDAY:

Date:

Speak to My Heart, Lord

THURSDAY:

Date:

FRIDAY:

Date:

SATURDAY:

Date:

Sunday Service
A Light for My Path

WEEK FIVE

I was glad when they said to me,
"Let us go into the house of the Lord."

Psalm 122:1 (NKJV)

Date: _____ Speaker: _____

Sermon Title: _____

Scripture Text: _____

Notes:

_____
_____
_____
_____
_____
_____
_____
_____
_____
_____
_____
_____

Praise Reports

The Week in Review

WEEK FIVE

*Come and see what our God has done,
what awesome miracles he performs for people!*

Psalm 66:5 (NLT)

This Week's Prayer List

I urge you, first of all, to pray for all people. Ask God to help them; intercede on their behalf, and give thanks for them.

1 Timothy 2:1 (NLT)

Name: _____

Date: _____

Prayer Request:
_____
_____
_____
_____

Name: _____

Date: _____

Prayer Request:
_____
_____
_____
_____

My Personal Prayer Requests

Delight yourself also in the Lord, and He shall give you the desires of your heart. Commit your way to the Lord, trust also in Him, and He shall bring it to pass.

Psalm 37:4–5 (**NKJV**)

Date: _____

Prayer Request:

_____
_____
_____
_____
_____
_____
_____
_____

Scripture Promise:

_____
_____
_____

Quiet Moments with You
Daily Devotions

WEEK SIX

*Then the Lord came and stood and called as at other times,
"Samuel! Samuel!" And Samuel answered,
"Speak, for Your servant hears."*

1 Samuel 3:10 (NKJV)

MONDAY:

Date:

_____
_____
_____
_____
_____
_____
_____
_____
_____
_____
_____
_____
_____
_____

TUESDAY:

Date:

WEDNESDAY:

Date:

Speak to My Heart, Lord

THURSDAY:

Date:

FRIDAY:

Date:

SATURDAY:

Date:

Sunday Service

A Light for My Path

WEEK SIX

I was glad when they said to me,
"Let us go into the house of the Lord."

Psalm 122:1 (**NKJV**)

Date: _____ Speaker: _____

Sermon Title: _____

Scripture Text: _____

Notes:

_____
_____
_____
_____
_____
_____
_____
_____
_____
_____
_____
_____

Praise Reports

The Week in Review

WEEK SIX

*Come and see what our God has done,
what awesome miracles he performs for people!*

Psalm 66:5 (NLT)

This Week's Prayer List
Week Seven

I urge you, first of all, to pray for all people. Ask God to help them; intercede on their behalf, and give thanks for them.

1 Timothy 2:1 (NLT)

Name: _____

Date: _____

Prayer Request:

_____
_____
_____
_____

Name: _____

Date: _____

Prayer Request:

_____
_____
_____
_____

My Personal Prayer Requests
Week Seven

Delight yourself also in the Lord, and He shall give you the desires of your heart. Commit your way to the Lord, trust also in Him, and He shall bring it to pass.

Psalm 37:4–5 (NKJV)

Date: _____

Prayer Request:

_____
_____
_____
_____
_____
_____
_____
_____

Scripture Promise:

_____
_____
_____

Quiet Moments with You
Daily Devotions

WEEK SEVEN

Then the Lord came and stood and called as at other times, "Samuel! Samuel!" And Samuel answered, "Speak, for Your servant hears."

1 Samuel 3:10 (NKJV)

MONDAY:

Date:

TUESDAY:

Date:

WEDNESDAY:

Date:

Speak to My Heart, Lord

THURSDAY:

Date:

FRIDAY:

Date:

SATURDAY:

Date:

Sunday Service

A Light for My Path

WEEK SEVEN

*I was glad when they said to me,
"Let us go into the house of the Lord."*

Psalm 122:1 (NKJV)

Date: _____ Speaker: _____

Sermon Title: _____

Scripture Text: _____

Notes:

_____
_____
_____
_____
_____
_____
_____
_____
_____
_____
_____
_____

Praise Reports

The Week in Review

WEEK SEVEN

*Come and see what our God has done,
what awesome miracles he performs for people!*

Psalm 66:5 (NLT)

This Week's Prayer List
Week Eight

I urge you, first of all, to pray for all people. Ask God to help them; intercede on their behalf, and give thanks for them.

1 Timothy 2:1 (NLT)

Name: _____

Date: _____

Prayer Request:
_____
_____
_____
_____

Name: _____

Date: _____

Prayer Request:
_____
_____
_____
_____

My Personal Prayer Requests
Week Eight

Delight yourself also in the Lord, and He shall give you the desires of your heart. Commit your way to the Lord, trust also in Him, and He shall bring it to pass.

Psalm 37:4–5 (**NKJV**)

Date: _____

Prayer Request:

Scripture Promise:

Quiet Moments with You
Daily Devotions

WEEK EIGHT

*Then the Lord came and stood and called as at other times,
"Samuel! Samuel!" And Samuel answered,
"Speak, for Your servant hears."*

1 Samuel 3:10 (NKJV)

MONDAY:

Date:

TUESDAY:

Date:

WEDNESDAY:

Date:

Speak to My Heart, Lord

THURSDAY:

Date:

FRIDAY:

Date:

SATURDAY:

Date:

Sunday Service

A Light for My Path

WEEK EIGHT

I was glad when they said to me,
"Let us go into the house of the Lord."

Psalm 122:1 (**NKJV**)

Date: _____ Speaker: _____

Sermon Title: _____

Scripture Text: _____

Notes:

_____
_____
_____
_____
_____
_____
_____
_____
_____
_____

Praise Reports

The Week in Review

WEEK EIGHT

*Come and see what our God has done,
what awesome miracles he performs for people!*

Psalm 66:5 (NLT)

This Week's Prayer List
Week Nine

I urge you, first of all, to pray for all people. Ask God to help them; intercede on their behalf, and give thanks for them.

1 Timothy 2:1 (NLT)

Name: _____

Date: _____

Prayer Request:

_____
_____
_____
_____

Name: _____

Date: _____

Prayer Request:

_____
_____
_____
_____

My Personal Prayer Requests
Week Nine

Delight yourself also in the Lord, and He shall give you the desires of your heart. Commit your way to the Lord, trust also in Him, and He shall bring it to pass.

Psalm 37:4–5 (**NKJV**)

Date: _____

Prayer Request:

_____
_____
_____
_____
_____
_____
_____
_____

Scripture Promise:

_____
_____
_____

Quiet Moments with You
Daily Devotions

WEEK NINE

*Then the Lord came and stood and called as at other times,
"Samuel! Samuel!" And Samuel answered,
"Speak, for Your servant hears."*

1 Samuel 3:10 (**NKJV**)

MONDAY:

Date:

TUESDAY:

Date:

WEDNESDAY:

Date:

Speak to My Heart, Lord

THURSDAY:

Date:

FRIDAY:

Date:

SATURDAY:

Date:

Sunday Service
A Light for My Path

WEEK NINE

*I was glad when they said to me,
"Let us go into the house of the Lord."*

Psalm 122:1 (**NKJV**)

Date: _____ Speaker: _____

Sermon Title: _____

Scripture Text: _____

Notes:

_____
_____
_____
_____
_____
_____
_____
_____
_____
_____
_____
_____

Praise Reports

The Week in Review

WEEK NINE

*Come and see what our God has done,
what awesome miracles he performs for people!*

Psalm 66:5 (NLT)

This Week's Prayer List
Week Ten

I urge you, first of all, to pray for all people. Ask God to help them; intercede on their behalf, and give thanks for them.

1 Timothy 2:1 (NLT)

Name: _____

Date: _____

Prayer Request:
_____
_____
_____
_____

Name: _____

Date: _____

Prayer Request:
_____
_____
_____
_____

My Personal Prayer Requests
Week Ten

Delight yourself also in the Lord, and He shall give you the desires of your heart. Commit your way to the Lord, trust also in Him, and He shall bring it to pass.

Psalm 37:4–5 (NKJV)

Date: _____

Prayer Request:

_____
_____
_____
_____
_____
_____
_____
_____
_____

Scripture Promise:

_____
_____
_____

Quiet Moments with You
Daily Devotions

WEEK TEN

*Then the Lord came and stood and called as at other times,
"Samuel! Samuel!" And Samuel answered,
"Speak, for Your servant hears."*

1 Samuel 3:10 (**NKJV**)

MONDAY:

Date:

___
___
___
___
___
___
___
___
___
___
___
___

TUESDAY:

Date:

WEDNESDAY:

Date:

Speak to My Heart, Lord

THURSDAY:

Date:

FRIDAY:

Date:

SATURDAY:

Date:

Sunday Service

A Light for My Path

WEEK TEN

I was glad when they said to me,
"Let us go into the house of the Lord."

Psalm 122:1 (NKJV)

Date: _____ Speaker: _____

Sermon Title: _____

Scripture Text: _____

Notes:

_____
_____
_____
_____
_____
_____
_____
_____
_____
_____
_____

Praise Reports

The Week in Review

WEEK TEN

*Come and see what our God has done,
what awesome miracles he performs for people!*

Psalm 66:5 (NLT)

This Week's Prayer List
Week Eleven

I urge you, first of all, to pray for all people. Ask God to help them; intercede on their behalf, and give thanks for them.

1 Timothy 2:1 (NLT)

Name: _____

Date: _____

Prayer Request:

_____
_____
_____
_____

Name: _____

Date: _____

Prayer Request:

_____
_____
_____
_____

My Personal Prayer Requests
Week Eleven

Delight yourself also in the Lord, and He shall give you the desires of your heart. Commit your way to the Lord, trust also in Him, and He shall bring it to pass.

Psalm 37:4–5 (NKJV)

Date: _____

Prayer Request:

_____
_____
_____
_____
_____
_____
_____
_____
_____

Scripture Promise:

_____
_____
_____

Quiet Moments with You
Daily Devotions

WEEK ELEVEN

Then the Lord came and stood and called as at other times, "Samuel! Samuel!" And Samuel answered, "Speak, for Your servant hears."

1 Samuel 3:10 (NKJV)

MONDAY:

Date:

TUESDAY:

Date:

WEDNESDAY:

Date:

Speak to My Heart, Lord

THURSDAY:

Date:

FRIDAY:

Date:

SATURDAY:

Date:

Sunday Service
A Light for My Path

WEEK ELEVEN

I was glad when they said to me,
"Let us go into the house of the Lord."

Psalm 122:1 (**NKJV**)

Date: _____ Speaker: _____

Sermon Title: _____

Scripture Text: _____

Notes:

_____
_____
_____
_____
_____
_____
_____
_____
_____
_____
_____

Praise Reports

The Week in Review

WEEK ELEVEN

*Come and see what our God has done,
what awesome miracles he performs for people!*

Psalm 66:5 (NLT)

This Week's Prayer List
Week Twelve

I urge you, first of all, to pray for all people. Ask God to help them; intercede on their behalf, and give thanks for them.

1 Timothy 2:1 (NLT)

Name: _____

Date: _____

Prayer Request:
_____
_____
_____
_____

Name: _____

Date: _____

Prayer Request:
_____
_____
_____
_____

My Personal Prayer Requests

Week Twelve

Delight yourself also in the Lord, and He shall give you the desires of your heart. Commit your way to the Lord, trust also in Him, and He shall bring it to pass.

Psalm 37:4–5 (NKJV)

Date: _____

Prayer Request:

_____
_____
_____
_____
_____
_____
_____
_____

Scripture Promise:

_____
_____
_____

Quiet Moments with You
Daily Devotions

WEEK TWELVE

*Then the Lord came and stood and called as at other times,
"Samuel! Samuel!" And Samuel answered,
"Speak, for Your servant hears."*

1 Samuel 3:10 (NKJV)

MONDAY:

Date:

_____
_____
_____
_____
_____
_____
_____
_____
_____
_____
_____

TUESDAY:

Date:

WEDNESDAY:

Date:

Speak to My Heart, Lord

THURSDAY:

Date:

FRIDAY:

Date:

SATURDAY:

Date:

Sunday Service
A Light for My Path

WEEK TWELVE

I was glad when they said to me,
"Let us go into the house of the Lord."

Psalm 122:1 (**NKJV**)

Date: _____ Speaker: _____

Sermon Title: _____

Scripture Text: _____

Notes:

_____
_____
_____
_____
_____
_____
_____
_____
_____
_____
_____

Praise Reports

The Week in Review

WEEK TWELVE

*Come and see what our God has done,
what awesome miracles he performs for people!*

Psalm 66:5 (NLT)

This Week's Prayer List
Week Thirteen

I urge you, first of all, to pray for all people. Ask God to help them; intercede on their behalf, and give thanks for them.

1 Timothy 2:1 (NLT)

Name: _____

Date: _____

Prayer Request:

_____
_____
_____
_____

Name: _____

Date: _____

Prayer Request:

_____
_____
_____
_____

My Personal Prayer Requests
Week Thirteen

Delight yourself also in the Lord, and He shall give you the desires of your heart. Commit your way to the Lord, trust also in Him, and He shall bring it to pass.

Psalm 37:4–5 (**NKJV**)

Date: _____

Prayer Request:

_____
_____
_____
_____
_____
_____
_____
_____

Scripture Promise:

_____
_____
_____

Quiet Moments with You
Daily Devotions

WEEK THIRTEEN

Then the Lord came and stood and called as at other times, "Samuel! Samuel!" And Samuel answered, "Speak, for Your servant hears."

1 Samuel 3:10 (NKJV)

MONDAY:

Date:

TUESDAY:

Date:

WEDNESDAY:

Date:

Speak to My Heart, Lord

THURSDAY:

Date:

FRIDAY:

Date:

SATURDAY:

Date:

Sunday Service

A Light for My Path

WEEK THIRTEEN

*I was glad when they said to me,
"Let us go into the house of the Lord."*

Psalm 122:1 (NKJV)

Date: _____ Speaker: _____

Sermon Title: _____

Scripture Text: _____

Notes:

_____
_____
_____
_____
_____
_____
_____
_____
_____
_____
_____

Praise Reports

The Week in Review

WEEK THIRTEEN

Come and see what our God has done,
what awesome miracles he performs for people!

Psalm 66:5 (NLT)

This Week's Prayer List
Week Fourteen

I urge you, first of all, to pray for all people. Ask God to help them; intercede on their behalf, and give thanks for them.

1 Timothy 2:1 (NLT)

Name: _____

Date: _____

Prayer Request:
_____
_____
_____
_____

Name: _____

Date: _____

Prayer Request:
_____
_____
_____
_____

My Personal Prayer Requests
Week Fourteen

Delight yourself also in the Lord, and He shall give you the desires of your heart. Commit your way to the Lord, trust also in Him, and He shall bring it to pass.

Psalm 37:4–5 (**NKJV**)

Date: _____

Prayer Request:

_____
_____
_____
_____
_____
_____
_____
_____

Scripture Promise:

_____
_____
_____

Quiet Moments with You
Daily Devotions

WEEK FOURTEEN

Then the Lord came and stood and called as at other times, "Samuel! Samuel!" And Samuel answered, "Speak, for Your servant hears."

1 Samuel 3:10 (NKJV)

MONDAY:

Date:

TUESDAY:

Date:

WEDNESDAY:

Date:

Speak to My Heart, Lord

THURSDAY:

Date:

FRIDAY:

Date:

SATURDAY:

Date:

Sunday Service

A Light for My Path

WEEK FOURTEEN

*I was glad when they said to me,
"Let us go into the house of the Lord."*

Psalm 122:1 (**NKJV**)

Date: _____ Speaker: _____

Sermon Title: _____

Scripture Text: _____

Notes:

_____
_____
_____
_____
_____
_____
_____
_____
_____
_____

Praise Reports

The Week in Review

WEEK FOURTEEN

*Come and see what our God has done,
what awesome miracles he performs for people!*

Psalm 66:5 (NLT)

This Week's Prayer List

Week Fifteen

I urge you, first of all, to pray for all people. Ask God to help them; intercede on their behalf, and give thanks for them.

1 Timothy 2:1 (NLT)

Name: _____

Date: _____

Prayer Request:

_____
_____
_____
_____

Name: _____

Date: _____

Prayer Request:

_____
_____
_____
_____

My Personal Prayer Requests
Week Fifteen

Delight yourself also in the Lord, and He shall give you the desires of your heart. Commit your way to the Lord, trust also in Him, and He shall bring it to pass.

Psalm 37:4–5 (**NKJV**)

Date: _____

Prayer Request:

_____
_____
_____
_____
_____
_____
_____
_____

Scripture Promise:

_____
_____
_____

Quiet Moments with You
Daily Devotions

WEEK FIFTEEN

Then the Lord came and stood and called as at other times, "Samuel! Samuel!" And Samuel answered, "Speak, for Your servant hears."

1 Samuel 3:10 (**NKJV**)

MONDAY:

Date:

TUESDAY:

Date:

WEDNESDAY:

Date:

Speak to My Heart, Lord

THURSDAY:

Date:

FRIDAY:

Date:

SATURDAY:

Date:

Sunday Service
A Light for My Path

WEEK FIFTEEN

I was glad when they said to me,
"Let us go into the house of the Lord."

Psalm 122:1 (**NKJV**)

Date: _____ Speaker: _____

Sermon Title: _____

Scripture Text: _____

Notes:

_____
_____
_____
_____
_____
_____
_____
_____
_____
_____

Praise Reports

The Week in Review

WEEK FIFTEEN

*Come and see what our God has done,
what awesome miracles he performs for people!*

Psalm 66:5 (NLT)

This Week's Prayer List
Week Sixteen

I urge you, first of all, to pray for all people. Ask God to help them; intercede on their behalf, and give thanks for them.

1 Timothy 2:1 (NLT)

Name: _____

Date: _____

Prayer Request:
_____
_____
_____
_____

Name: _____

Date: _____

Prayer Request:
_____
_____
_____
_____

My Personal Prayer Requests
Week Sixteen

Delight yourself also in the Lord, and He shall give you the desires of your heart. Commit your way to the Lord, trust also in Him, and He shall bring it to pass.

Psalm 37:4–5 (NKJV)

Date:

Prayer Request:

Scripture Promise:

Quiet Moments with You
Daily Devotions

WEEK SIXTEEN

Then the Lord came and stood and called as at other times, "Samuel! Samuel!" And Samuel answered, "Speak, for Your servant hears."

1 Samuel 3:10 (**NKJV**)

MONDAY:

Date:

TUESDAY:

Date:

WEDNESDAY:

Date:

Speak to My Heart, Lord

THURSDAY:

Date:

FRIDAY:

Date:

SATURDAY:

Date:

Sunday Service

A Light for My Path

WEEK SIXTEEN

I was glad when they said to me,
"Let us go into the house of the Lord."

Psalm 122:1 (NKJV)

Date: _____ Speaker: _____

Sermon Title: _____

Scripture Text: _____

Notes:

_____
_____
_____
_____
_____
_____
_____
_____
_____
_____
_____
_____

Praise Reports

The Week in Review

WEEK SIXTEEN

*Come and see what our God has done,
what awesome miracles he performs for people!*

Psalm 66:5 (NLT)

This Week's Prayer List
Week Seventeen

I urge you, first of all, to pray for all people. Ask God to help them; intercede on their behalf, and give thanks for them.

1 Timothy 2:1 (NLT)

Name: _____

Date: _____

Prayer Request:
_____
_____
_____
_____

Name: _____

Date: _____

Prayer Request:
_____
_____
_____
_____

My Personal Prayer Requests
Week Seventeen

Delight yourself also in the Lord, and He shall give you the desires of your heart. Commit your way to the Lord, trust also in Him, and He shall bring it to pass.

Psalm 37:4–5 (**NKJV**)

Date: _____

Prayer Request:

_____
_____
_____
_____
_____
_____
_____
_____

Scripture Promise:

_____
_____
_____

Quiet Moments with You
Daily Devotions

WEEK SEVENTEEN

Then the Lord came and stood and called as at other times, "Samuel! Samuel!" And Samuel answered, "Speak, for Your servant hears."

1 Samuel 3:10 (**NKJV**)

MONDAY:

Date:

TUESDAY:

Date:

WEDNESDAY:

Date:

Speak to My Heart, Lord

THURSDAY:

Date:

FRIDAY:

Date:

SATURDAY:

Date:

Sunday Service

A Light for My Path

WEEK SEVENTEEN

I was glad when they said to me,
"Let us go into the house of the Lord."

Psalm 122:1 (NKJV)

Date: _____ Speaker: _____

Sermon Title: _____

Scripture Text: _____

Notes:

_____
_____
_____
_____
_____
_____
_____
_____
_____
_____
_____
_____

Praise Reports

The Week in Review

WEEK SEVENTEEN

*Come and see what our God has done,
what awesome miracles he performs for people!*

Psalm 66:5 (NLT)

This Week's Prayer List
Week Eighteen

I urge you, first of all, to pray for all people. Ask God to help them; intercede on their behalf, and give thanks for them.

1 Timothy 2:1 (NLT)

Name: _____

Date: _____

Prayer Request:
_____
_____
_____
_____

Name: _____

Date: _____

Prayer Request:
_____
_____
_____
_____

My Personal Prayer Requests
Week Eighteen

Delight yourself also in the Lord, and He shall give you the desires of your heart. Commit your way to the Lord, trust also in Him, and He shall bring it to pass.

Psalm 37:4–5 (NKJV)

Date: _____

Prayer Request:

_____
_____
_____
_____
_____
_____
_____
_____

Scripture Promise:

_____
_____
_____

Quiet Moments with You
Daily Devotions

WEEK EIGHTEEN

*Then the Lord came and stood and called as at other times,
"Samuel! Samuel!" And Samuel answered,
"Speak, for Your servant hears."*

1 Samuel 3:10 (NKJV)

MONDAY:

Date:

TUESDAY:

Date:

WEDNESDAY:

Date:

Speak to My Heart, Lord

THURSDAY:

Date:

FRIDAY:

Date:

SATURDAY:

Date:

Sunday Service
A Light for My Path

WEEK EIGHTEEN

I was glad when they said to me,
"Let us go into the house of the Lord."

Psalm 122:1 (**NKJV**)

Date: _____ Speaker: _____

Sermon Title: _____

Scripture Text: _____

Notes:

_____
_____
_____
_____
_____
_____
_____
_____
_____
_____

Praise Reports

The Week in Review

WEEK EIGHTEEN

*Come and see what our God has done,
what awesome miracles he performs for people!*

Psalm 66:5 (NLT)

This Week's Prayer List
Week Nineteen

I urge you, first of all, to pray for all people. Ask God to help them; intercede on their behalf, and give thanks for them.

1 Timothy 2:1 (NLT)

Name: _____

Date: _____

Prayer Request:
_____
_____
_____
_____

Name: _____

Date: _____

Prayer Request:
_____
_____
_____
_____

My Personal Prayer Requests
Week Nineteen

Delight yourself also in the Lord, and He shall give you the desires of your heart. Commit your way to the Lord, trust also in Him, and He shall bring it to pass.

Psalm 37:4–5 (NKJV)

Date: _____

Prayer Request:

_____
_____
_____
_____
_____
_____
_____
_____

Scripture Promise:

_____
_____
_____

Quiet Moments with You
Daily Devotions

WEEK NINETEEN

Then the Lord came and stood and called as at other times, "Samuel! Samuel!" And Samuel answered, "Speak, for Your servant hears."

1 Samuel 3:10 (NKJV)

MONDAY:

Date:

TUESDAY:

Date:

WEDNESDAY:

Date:

Speak to My Heart, Lord

THURSDAY:

Date:

FRIDAY:

Date:

SATURDAY:

Date:

Sunday Service
A Light for My Path

WEEK NINETEEN

*I was glad when they said to me,
"Let us go into the house of the Lord."*

Psalm 122:1 (**NKJV**)

Date: _____ Speaker: _____

Sermon Title: _____

Scripture Text: _____

Notes:

_____
_____
_____
_____
_____
_____
_____
_____
_____
_____

WEEK NINETEEN

Praise Reports

The Week in Review

WEEK NINETEEN

*Come and see what our God has done,
what awesome miracles he performs for people!*

Psalm 66:5 (NLT)

This Week's Prayer List
Week Twenty

I urge you, first of all, to pray for all people. Ask God to help them; intercede on their behalf, and give thanks for them.

1 Timothy 2:1 (NLT)

Name: _____

Date: _____

Prayer Request:
_____
_____
_____
_____

Name: _____

Date: _____

Prayer Request:
_____
_____
_____

My Personal Prayer Requests
Week Twenty

Delight yourself also in the Lord, and He shall give you the desires of your heart. Commit your way to the Lord, trust also in Him, and He shall bring it to pass.

Psalm 37:4–5 (**NKJV**)

Date: _____

Prayer Request:

_____
_____
_____
_____
_____
_____
_____
_____
_____

Scripture Promise:

_____
_____
_____

Quiet Moments with You
Daily Devotions

WEEK TWENTY

Then the Lord came and stood and called as at other times, "Samuel! Samuel!" And Samuel answered, "Speak, for Your servant hears."

1 Samuel 3:10 (NKJV)

MONDAY:

Date:

TUESDAY:

Date:

WEDNESDAY:

Date:

Speak to My Heart, Lord

THURSDAY:

Date:

FRIDAY:

Date:

SATURDAY:

Date:

Sunday Service

A Light for My Path

WEEK TWENTY

*I was glad when they said to me,
"Let us go into the house of the Lord."*

Psalm 122:1 (**NKJV**)

Date: _____ Speaker: _____

Sermon Title: _____

Scripture Text: _____

Notes:

_____
_____
_____
_____
_____
_____
_____
_____
_____
_____
_____
_____
_____

Praise Reports

The Week in Review

WEEK TWENTY

*Come and see what our God has done,
what awesome miracles he performs for people!*

Psalm 66:5 (NLT)

This Week's Prayer List

Week Twenty-One

I urge you, first of all, to pray for all people. Ask God to help them; intercede on their behalf, and give thanks for them.

1 Timothy 2:1 (NLT)

Name: _____

Date: _____

Prayer Request:

_____
_____
_____
_____

Name: _____

Date: _____

Prayer Request:

_____
_____
_____
_____

My Personal Prayer Requests
Week Twenty-One

Delight yourself also in the Lord, and He shall give you the desires of your heart. Commit your way to the Lord, trust also in Him, and He shall bring it to pass.

Psalm 37:4–5 (NKJV)

Date: _____

Prayer Request:

_____
_____
_____
_____
_____
_____
_____
_____

Scripture Promise:

_____
_____
_____

Quiet Moments with You
Daily Devotions

WEEK TWENTY-ONE

*Then the Lord came and stood and called as at other times,
"Samuel! Samuel!" And Samuel answered,
"Speak, for Your servant hears."*

1 Samuel 3:10 (**NKJV**)

MONDAY:

Date:

TUESDAY:

Date:

WEDNESDAY:

Date:

Speak to My Heart, Lord

THURSDAY:

Date:

FRIDAY:

Date:

SATURDAY:

Date:

Sunday Service

A Light for My Path

WEEK TWENTY-ONE

I was glad when they said to me,
"Let us go into the house of the Lord."

Psalm 122:1 (**NKJV**)

Date: _____ Speaker: _____

Sermon Title: _____

Scripture Text: _____

Notes:

_____
_____
_____
_____
_____
_____
_____
_____
_____
_____

Praise Reports

The Week in Review

WEEK TWENTY-ONE

*Come and see what our God has done,
what awesome miracles he performs for people!*

Psalm 66:5 (NLT)

This Week's Prayer List

Week Twenty-Two

I urge you, first of all, to pray for all people. Ask God to help them; intercede on their behalf, and give thanks for them.

1 Timothy 2:1 (NLT)

Name: _____

Date: _____

Prayer Request:

_____
_____
_____
_____

Name: _____

Date: _____

Prayer Request:

_____
_____
_____
_____

My Personal Prayer Requests
Week Twenty-Two

Delight yourself also in the Lord, and He shall give you the desires of your heart. Commit your way to the Lord, trust also in Him, and He shall bring it to pass.

Psalm 37:4–5 (NKJV)

Date: _____

Prayer Request:

_____
_____
_____
_____
_____
_____
_____
_____

Scripture Promise:

_____
_____
_____

Quiet Moments with You
Daily Devotions

WEEK TWENTY-TWO

Then the Lord came and stood and called as at other times,
"Samuel! Samuel!" And Samuel answered,
"Speak, for Your servant hears."

1 Samuel 3:10 (**NKJV**)

MONDAY:

Date:

TUESDAY:

Date:

WEDNESDAY:

Date:

Speak to My Heart, Lord

THURSDAY:

Date:

FRIDAY:

Date:

SATURDAY:

Date:

Sunday Service
A Light for My Path

WEEK TWENTY-TWO

I was glad when they said to me,
"Let us go into the house of the Lord."

Psalm 122:1 (NKJV)

Date: _____ Speaker: _____

Sermon Title: _____

Scripture Text: _____

Notes:

_____
_____
_____
_____
_____
_____
_____
_____
_____
_____
_____

Praise Reports

The Week in Review

WEEK TWENTY-TWO

*Come and see what our God has done,
what awesome miracles he performs for people!*

Psalm 66:5 (NLT)

This Week's Prayer List
Week Twenty-Three

I urge you, first of all, to pray for all people. Ask God to help them; intercede on their behalf, and give thanks for them.

1 Timothy 2:1 (NLT)

Name: _____

Date: _____

Prayer Request:

_____
_____
_____
_____

Name: _____

Date: _____

Prayer Request:

_____
_____
_____
_____

My Personal Prayer Requests
Week Twenty-Three

Delight yourself also in the Lord, and He shall give you the desires of your heart. Commit your way to the Lord, trust also in Him, and He shall bring it to pass.

Psalm 37:4–5 (NKJV)

Date: _____

Prayer Request:

_____
_____
_____
_____
_____
_____
_____
_____
_____

Scripture Promise:

_____
_____
_____

Quiet Moments with You
Daily Devotions

WEEK TWENTY-THREE

*Then the Lord came and stood and called as at other times,
"Samuel! Samuel!" And Samuel answered,
"Speak, for Your servant hears."*

1 Samuel 3:10 (NKJV)

MONDAY:

Date:

TUESDAY:

Date:

WEDNESDAY:

Date:

Speak to My Heart, Lord

THURSDAY:

Date:

FRIDAY:

Date:

SATURDAY:

Date:

Sunday Service

A Light for My Path

WEEK TWENTY-THREE

*I was glad when they said to me,
"Let us go into the house of the Lord."*

Psalm 122:1 (NKJV)

Date: _____ Speaker: _____

Sermon Title: _____

Scripture Text: _____

Notes:

_____
_____
_____
_____
_____
_____
_____
_____
_____
_____
_____

Praise Reports

The Week in Review

WEEK TWENTY-THREE

*Come and see what our God has done,
what awesome miracles he performs for people!*

Psalm 66:5 (NLT)

This Week's Prayer List
Week Twenty-Four

I urge you, first of all, to pray for all people. Ask God to help them; intercede on their behalf, and give thanks for them.

1 Timothy 2:1 (NLT)

Name: _____

Date: _____

Prayer Request:

_____
_____
_____
_____

Name: _____

Date: _____

Prayer Request:

_____
_____
_____
_____

My Personal Prayer Requests
Week Twenty-Four

Delight yourself also in the Lord, and He shall give you the desires of your heart. Commit your way to the Lord, trust also in Him, and He shall bring it to pass.

Psalm 37:4–5 (NKJV)

Date: _____

Prayer Request:

_____
_____
_____
_____
_____
_____
_____
_____

Scripture Promise:

_____
_____
_____

Quiet Moments with You
Daily Devotions

WEEK TWENTY-FOUR

*Then the Lord came and stood and called as at other times,
"Samuel! Samuel!" And Samuel answered,
"Speak, for Your servant hears."*

1 Samuel 3:10 (NKJV)

MONDAY:

Date:

TUESDAY:

Date:

WEDNESDAY:

Date:

Speak to My Heart, Lord

THURSDAY:

Date:

FRIDAY:

Date:

SATURDAY:

Date:

Sunday Service

A Light for My Path

WEEK TWENTY-FOUR

I was glad when they said to me,
"Let us go into the house of the Lord."

Psalm 122:1 (**NKJV**)

Date: _____ Speaker: _____

Sermon Title: _____

Scripture Text: _____

Notes:

_____
_____
_____
_____
_____
_____
_____
_____
_____
_____

Praise Reports

THE WEEK IN REVIEW

WEEK TWENTY-FOUR

*Come and see what our God has done,
what awesome miracles he performs for people!*

Psalm 66:5 (NLT)

This Week's Prayer List
Week Twenty-Five

I urge you, first of all, to pray for all people. Ask God to help them; intercede on their behalf, and give thanks for them.

1 Timothy 2:1 (NLT)

Name: _____

Date: _____

Prayer Request:

_____
_____
_____
_____

Name: _____

Date: _____

Prayer Request:

_____
_____
_____
_____

My Personal Prayer Requests
Week Twenty-Five

Delight yourself also in the Lord, and He shall give you the desires of your heart. Commit your way to the Lord, trust also in Him, and He shall bring it to pass.

Psalm 37:4–5 (NKJV)

Date: _____

Prayer Request:

_____
_____
_____
_____
_____
_____
_____
_____

Scripture Promise:

_____
_____
_____

Quiet Moments with You
Daily Devotions

WEEK TWENTY-FIVE

*Then the Lord came and stood and called as at other times,
"Samuel! Samuel!" And Samuel answered,
"Speak, for Your servant hears."*

1 Samuel 3:10 (NKJV)

MONDAY:

Date:

TUESDAY:

Date:

WEDNESDAY:

Date:

Speak to My Heart, Lord

THURSDAY:

Date:

FRIDAY:

Date:

SATURDAY:

Date:

Sunday Service
A Light for My Path

WEEK TWENTY-FIVE

I was glad when they said to me,
"Let us go into the house of the Lord."

Psalm 122:1 (**NKJV**)

Date: _____ Speaker: _____

Sermon Title: _____

Scripture Text: _____

Notes:

_____
_____
_____
_____
_____
_____
_____
_____
_____
_____
_____

Praise Reports

The Week in Review

WEEK TWENTY-FIVE

*Come and see what our God has done,
what awesome miracles he performs for people!*

Psalm 66:5 (NLT)

This Week's Prayer List
Week Twenty-Six

I urge you, first of all, to pray for all people. Ask God to help them; intercede on their behalf, and give thanks for them.

1 Timothy 2:1 (NLT)

Name: _____

Date: _____

Prayer Request:
_____
_____
_____
_____

Name: _____

Date: _____

Prayer Request:
_____
_____
_____
_____

My Personal Prayer Requests
Week Twenty-Six

Delight yourself also in the Lord, and He shall give you the desires of your heart. Commit your way to the Lord, trust also in Him, and He shall bring it to pass.

Psalm 37:4–5 (**NKJV**)

Date:

Prayer Request:

Scripture Promise:

Quiet Moments with You
Daily Devotions

WEEK TWENTY-SIX

Then the Lord came and stood and called as at other times, "Samuel! Samuel!" And Samuel answered, "Speak, for Your servant hears."

1 Samuel 3:10 (NKJV)

MONDAY:

Date:

TUESDAY:

Date:

WEDNESDAY:

Date:

Speak to My Heart, Lord

THURSDAY:

Date:

FRIDAY:

Date:

SATURDAY:

Date:

Sunday Service
A Light for My Path

WEEK TWENTY-SIX

I was glad when they said to me,
"Let us go into the house of the Lord."

Psalm 122:1 (**NKJV**)

Date: _____ Speaker: _____

Sermon Title: _____

Scripture Text: _____

Notes:

_____
_____
_____
_____
_____
_____
_____
_____
_____
_____

Praise Reports

The Week in Review

WEEK TWENTY-SIX

*Come and see what our God has done,
what awesome miracles he performs for people!*

Psalm 66:5 (NLT)

This Week's Prayer List

Week Twenty-Seven

I urge you, first of all, to pray for all people. Ask God to help them; intercede on their behalf, and give thanks for them.

1 Timothy 2:1 (NLT)

Name: _____

Date: _____

Prayer Request:

_____

_____

_____

_____

Name: _____

Date: _____

Prayer Request:

_____

_____

_____

_____

My Personal Prayer Requests
Week Twenty-Seven

Delight yourself also in the Lord, and He shall give you the desires of your heart. Commit your way to the Lord, trust also in Him, and He shall bring it to pass.

Psalm 37:4–5 (NKJV)

Date: _____

Prayer Request:

_____
_____
_____
_____
_____
_____
_____
_____
_____

Scripture Promise:

_____
_____
_____

Quiet Moments with You
Daily Devotions

WEEK TWENTY-SEVEN

Then the Lord came and stood and called as at other times, "Samuel! Samuel!" And Samuel answered, "Speak, for Your servant hears."

1 Samuel 3:10 (**NKJV**)

MONDAY:

Date:

TUESDAY:

Date:

WEDNESDAY:

Date:

Speak to My Heart, Lord

THURSDAY:

Date:

FRIDAY:

Date:

SATURDAY:

Date:

Sunday Service
A Light for My Path

WEEK TWENTY-SEVEN

*I was glad when they said to me,
"Let us go into the house of the Lord."*

Psalm 122:1 (**NKJV**)

Date: _____ Speaker: _____

Sermon Title: _____

Scripture Text: _____

Notes:

_____
_____
_____
_____
_____
_____
_____
_____
_____
_____
_____
_____

Praise Reports

The Week in Review

WEEK TWENTY-SEVEN

*Come and see what our God has done,
what awesome miracles he performs for people!*

Psalm 66:5 (NLT)

THIS WEEK'S PRAYER LIST
Week Twenty-Eight

I urge you, first of all, to pray for all people. Ask God to help them; intercede on their behalf, and give thanks for them.

1 Timothy 2:1 (NLT)

Name: _____

Date: _____

Prayer Request:
_____
_____
_____
_____

Name: _____

Date: _____

Prayer Request:
_____
_____
_____
_____

My Personal Prayer Requests
Week Twenty-Eight

Delight yourself also in the Lord, and He shall give you the desires of your heart. Commit your way to the Lord, trust also in Him, and He shall bring it to pass.

Psalm 37:4–5 (**NKJV**)

Date: _____

Prayer Request:

_____
_____
_____
_____
_____
_____
_____
_____
_____

Scripture Promise:

_____
_____
_____

Quiet Moments with You
Daily Devotions

WEEK TWENTY-EIGHT

Then the Lord came and stood and called as at other times, "Samuel! Samuel!" And Samuel answered, "Speak, for Your servant hears."

1 Samuel 3:10 (**NKJV**)

MONDAY:

Date:

TUESDAY:

Date:

WEDNESDAY:

Date:

Speak to My Heart, Lord

THURSDAY:

Date:

FRIDAY:

Date:

SATURDAY:

Date:

Sunday Service
A Light for My Path

WEEK TWENTY-EIGHT

I was glad when they said to me,
"Let us go into the house of the Lord."

Psalm 122:1 (NKJV)

Date: _____ Speaker: _____

Sermon Title: _____

Scripture Text: _____

Notes:

_____
_____
_____
_____
_____
_____
_____
_____
_____
_____

Praise Reports

The Week in Review

WEEK TWENTY-EIGHT

*Come and see what our God has done,
what awesome miracles he performs for people!*

Psalm 66:5 (NLT)

This Week's Prayer List
Week Twenty-Nine

I urge you, first of all, to pray for all people. Ask God to help them; intercede on their behalf, and give thanks for them.

1 Timothy 2:1 (NLT)

Name: _____

Date: _____

Prayer Request:

_____
_____
_____
_____

Name: _____

Date: _____

Prayer Request:

_____
_____
_____
_____

My Personal Prayer Requests
Week Twenty-Nine

Delight yourself also in the Lord, and He shall give you the desires of your heart. Commit your way to the Lord, trust also in Him, and He shall bring it to pass.

Psalm 37:4–5 (NKJV)

Date: _____

Prayer Request:

_____
_____
_____
_____
_____
_____
_____
_____
_____

Scripture Promise:

_____
_____
_____

Quiet Moments with You
Daily Devotions

WEEK TWENTY-NINE

Then the Lord came and stood and called as at other times, "Samuel! Samuel!" And Samuel answered, "Speak, for Your servant hears."

1 Samuel 3:10 (**NKJV**)

MONDAY:

Date:

TUESDAY:

Date:

WEDNESDAY:

Date:

Speak to My Heart, Lord

THURSDAY:

Date:

FRIDAY:

Date:

SATURDAY:

Date:

Sunday Service
A Light for My Path

WEEK TWENTY-NINE

I was glad when they said to me,
"Let us go into the house of the Lord."

Psalm 122:1 (NKJV)

Date: _____ Speaker: _____

Sermon Title: _____

Scripture Text: _____

Notes:

_____
_____
_____
_____
_____
_____
_____
_____
_____
_____
_____

Praise Reports

The Week in Review

WEEK TWENTY-NINE

*Come and see what our God has done,
what awesome miracles he performs for people!*

Psalm 66:5 (NLT)

This Week's Prayer List
Week Thirty

I urge you, first of all, to pray for all people. Ask God to help them; intercede on their behalf, and give thanks for them.

1 Timothy 2:1 (NLT)

Name: _____

Date: _____

Prayer Request:

_____
_____
_____
_____

Name: _____

Date: _____

Prayer Request:

_____
_____
_____
_____

My Personal Prayer Requests
Week Thirty

Delight yourself also in the Lord, and He shall give you the desires of your heart. Commit your way to the Lord, trust also in Him, and He shall bring it to pass.

Psalm 37:4–5 (**NKJV**)

Date: _____

Prayer Request:

_____
_____
_____
_____
_____
_____
_____
_____
_____

Scripture Promise:

_____
_____
_____

Quiet Moments with You
Daily Devotions

WEEK THIRTY

Then the Lord came and stood and called as at other times,
"Samuel! Samuel!" And Samuel answered,
"Speak, for Your servant hears."

1 Samuel 3:10 (NKJV)

MONDAY:

Date:

TUESDAY:

Date:

WEDNESDAY:

Date:

Speak to My Heart, Lord

THURSDAY:

Date:

FRIDAY:

Date:

SATURDAY:

Date:

Sunday Service

A Light for My Path

WEEK THIRTY

I was glad when they said to me,
"Let us go into the house of the Lord."

Psalm 122:1 (**NKJV**)

Date: _____ Speaker: _____

Sermon Title: _____

Scripture Text: _____

Notes:

_____
_____
_____
_____
_____
_____
_____
_____
_____
_____

Praise Reports

The Week in Review

WEEK THIRTY

*Come and see what our God has done,
what awesome miracles he performs for people!*

Psalm 66:5 (NLT)

This Week's Prayer List
Week Thirty-One

I urge you, first of all, to pray for all people. Ask God to help them; intercede on their behalf, and give thanks for them.

1 Timothy 2:1 (NLT)

Name: _____

Date: _____

Prayer Request:

_____
_____
_____
_____

Name: _____

Date: _____

Prayer Request:

_____
_____
_____
_____

My Personal Prayer Requests
Week Thirty-One

Delight yourself also in the Lord, and He shall give you the desires of your heart. Commit your way to the Lord, trust also in Him, and He shall bring it to pass.

Psalm 37:4–5 (NKJV)

Date: _____

Prayer Request:

_____
_____
_____
_____
_____
_____
_____
_____
_____

Scripture Promise:

_____
_____
_____

Quiet Moments with You
Daily Devotions

WEEK THIRTY-ONE

Then the Lord came and stood and called as at other times,
"Samuel! Samuel!" And Samuel answered,
"Speak, for Your servant hears."

1 Samuel 3:10 (NKJV)

MONDAY:

Date:

TUESDAY:

Date:

WEDNESDAY:

Date:

Speak to My Heart, Lord

THURSDAY:

Date:

FRIDAY:

Date:

SATURDAY:

Date:

Sunday Service

A Light for My Path

WEEK THIRTY-ONE

I was glad when they said to me,
"Let us go into the house of the Lord."

Psalm 122:1 (**NKJV**)

Date: _____ Speaker: _____

Sermon Title: _____

Scripture Text: _____

Notes:

_____
_____
_____
_____
_____
_____
_____
_____
_____
_____

Praise Reports

The Week in Review

WEEK THIRTY-ONE

*Come and see what our God has done,
what awesome miracles he performs for people!*

Psalm 66:5 (NLT)

This Week's Prayer List
Week Thirty-Two

I urge you, first of all, to pray for all people. Ask God to help them; intercede on their behalf, and give thanks for them.

1 Timothy 2:1 (NLT)

Name: _____

Date: _____

Prayer Request:
_____
_____
_____
_____

Name: _____

Date: _____

Prayer Request:
_____
_____
_____
_____

My Personal Prayer Requests

Week Thirty-Two

Delight yourself also in the Lord, and He shall give you the desires of your heart. Commit your way to the Lord, trust also in Him, and He shall bring it to pass.

Psalm 37:4–5 (**NKJV**)

Date: _____

Prayer Request:

_____
_____
_____
_____
_____
_____
_____
_____
_____

Scripture Promise:

_____
_____
_____

Quiet Moments with You
Daily Devotions

WEEK THIRTY-TWO

Then the Lord came and stood and called as at other times, "Samuel! Samuel!" And Samuel answered, "Speak, for Your servant hears."

1 Samuel 3:10 (NKJV)

MONDAY:

Date:

TUESDAY:

Date:

WEDNESDAY:

Date:

Speak to My Heart, Lord

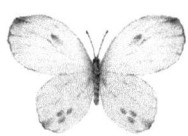

THURSDAY:

Date:

FRIDAY:

Date:

SATURDAY:

Date:

Sunday Service

A Light for My Path

WEEK THIRTY-TWO

I was glad when they said to me,
"Let us go into the house of the Lord."

Psalm 122:1 (NKJV)

Date: _____ Speaker: _____

Sermon Title: _____

Scripture Text: _____

Notes:

_____
_____
_____
_____
_____
_____
_____
_____
_____
_____

Praise Reports

The Week in Review

WEEK THIRTY-TWO

*Come and see what our God has done,
what awesome miracles he performs for people!*

Psalm 66:5 (**NLT**)

This Week's Prayer List
Week Thirty-Three

I urge you, first of all, to pray for all people. Ask God to help them; intercede on their behalf, and give thanks for them.

1 Timothy 2:1 (NLT)

Name: _____

Date: _____

Prayer Request:
_____
_____
_____
_____

Name: _____

Date: _____

Prayer Request:
_____
_____
_____
_____

My Personal Prayer Requests
Week Thirty-Three

Delight yourself also in the Lord, and He shall give you the desires of your heart. Commit your way to the Lord, trust also in Him, and He shall bring it to pass.

Psalm 37:4–5 (**NKJV**)

Date: _____

Prayer Request:

_____
_____
_____
_____
_____
_____
_____
_____
_____

Scripture Promise:

_____
_____
_____

Quiet Moments with You
Daily Devotions

WEEK THIRTY-THREE

*Then the Lord came and stood and called as at other times,
"Samuel! Samuel!" And Samuel answered,
"Speak, for Your servant hears."*

1 Samuel 3:10 (**NKJV**)

MONDAY:

Date:

TUESDAY:

Date:

_____
_____
_____
_____
_____
_____
_____

WEDNESDAY:

Date:

_____
_____
_____
_____
_____
_____
_____
_____

Speak to My Heart, Lord

THURSDAY:

Date:

FRIDAY:

Date:

SATURDAY:

Date:

Sunday Service

A Light for My Path

WEEK THIRTY-THREE

I was glad when they said to me,
"Let us go into the house of the Lord."

Psalm 122:1 (**NKJV**)

Date: _____ Speaker: _____

Sermon Title: _____

Scripture Text: _____

Notes:

_____
_____
_____
_____
_____
_____
_____
_____
_____
_____

Praise Reports

The Week in Review

WEEK THIRTY-THREE

*Come and see what our God has done,
what awesome miracles he performs for people!*

Psalm 66:5 (NLT)

This Week's Prayer List
Week Thirty-Four

I urge you, first of all, to pray for all people. Ask God to help them; intercede on their behalf, and give thanks for them.

1 Timothy 2:1 (NLT)

Name: _____

Date: _____

Prayer Request:

_____
_____
_____
_____

Name: _____

Date: _____

Prayer Request:

_____
_____
_____
_____

My Personal Prayer Requests
Week Thirty-Four

Delight yourself also in the Lord, and He shall give you the desires of your heart. Commit your way to the Lord, trust also in Him, and He shall bring it to pass.

Psalm 37:4–5 (NKJV)

Date: _____

Prayer Request:

_____
_____
_____
_____
_____
_____
_____
_____

Scripture Promise:

_____
_____
_____

Quiet Moments with You
Daily Devotions

WEEK THIRTY-FOUR

Then the Lord came and stood and called as at other times, "Samuel! Samuel!" And Samuel answered, "Speak, for Your servant hears."

1 Samuel 3:10 (**NKJV**)

MONDAY:

Date:

TUESDAY:

Date:

WEDNESDAY:

Date:

Speak to My Heart, Lord

THURSDAY:

Date:

FRIDAY:

Date:

SATURDAY:

Date:

Sunday Service

A Light for My Path

WEEK THIRTY-FOUR

I was glad when they said to me,
"Let us go into the house of the Lord."

Psalm 122:1 (**NKJV**)

Date: _____ Speaker: _____

Sermon Title: _____

Scripture Text: _____

Notes:

_____
_____
_____
_____
_____
_____
_____
_____
_____
_____
_____
_____

Praise Reports

The Week in Review

WEEK THIRTY-FOUR

*Come and see what our God has done,
what awesome miracles he performs for people!*

Psalm 66:5 (NLT)

This Week's Prayer List

Week Thirty-Five

I urge you, first of all, to pray for all people. Ask God to help them; intercede on their behalf, and give thanks for them.

1 Timothy 2:1 (NLT)

Name: _____

Date: _____

Prayer Request:
_____
_____
_____
_____

Name: _____

Date: _____

Prayer Request:
_____
_____
_____
_____

My Personal Prayer Requests
Week Thirty-Five

Delight yourself also in the Lord, and He shall give you the desires of your heart. Commit your way to the Lord, trust also in Him, and He shall bring it to pass.

Psalm 37:4–5 (NKJV)

Date: _____

Prayer Request:

_____
_____
_____
_____
_____
_____
_____
_____

Scripture Promise:

_____
_____
_____

Quiet Moments with You
Daily Devotions

WEEK THIRTY-FIVE

Then the Lord came and stood and called as at other times, "Samuel! Samuel!" And Samuel answered, "Speak, for Your servant hears."

1 Samuel 3:10 (**NKJV**)

MONDAY:

Date:

TUESDAY:

Date:

WEDNESDAY:

Date:

Speak to My Heart, Lord

THURSDAY:

Date:

FRIDAY:

Date:

SATURDAY:

Date:

Sunday Service
A Light for My Path

WEEK THIRTY-FIVE

I was glad when they said to me,
"Let us go into the house of the Lord."

Psalm 122:1 (NKJV)

Date: _____ Speaker: _____

Sermon Title: _____

Scripture Text: _____

Notes:

_____
_____
_____
_____
_____
_____
_____
_____
_____
_____
_____

Praise Reports

The Week in Review

WEEK THIRTY-FIVE

*Come and see what our God has done,
what awesome miracles he performs for people!*

Psalm 66:5 (NLT)

This Week's Prayer List
Week Thirty-Six

I urge you, first of all, to pray for all people. Ask God to help them; intercede on their behalf, and give thanks for them.

1 Timothy 2:1 (NLT)

Name: _____

Date: _____

Prayer Request:
_____
_____
_____
_____

Name: _____

Date: _____

Prayer Request:
_____
_____
_____
_____

My Personal Prayer Requests
Week Thirty-Six

Delight yourself also in the Lord, and He shall give you the desires of your heart. Commit your way to the Lord, trust also in Him, and He shall bring it to pass.

Psalm 37:4–5 (**NKJV**)

Date: _____

Prayer Request:

_____
_____
_____
_____
_____
_____
_____
_____
_____

Scripture Promise:

_____
_____
_____

Quiet Moments with You
Daily Devotions

WEEK THIRTY-SIX

*Then the Lord came and stood and called as at other times,
"Samuel! Samuel!" And Samuel answered,
"Speak, for Your servant hears."*

1 Samuel 3:10 (NKJV)

MONDAY:

Date:

_____
_____
_____
_____
_____
_____
_____
_____
_____
_____
_____
_____

TUESDAY:

Date:

WEDNESDAY:

Date:

Speak to My Heart, Lord

THURSDAY:

Date:

FRIDAY:

Date:

SATURDAY:

Date:

Sunday Service
A Light for My Path

WEEK THIRTY-SIX

I was glad when they said to me,
"Let us go into the house of the Lord."

Psalm 122:1 (**NKJV**)

Date: _____ Speaker: _____

Sermon Title: _____

Scripture Text: _____

Notes:

_____
_____
_____
_____
_____
_____
_____
_____
_____
_____

Praise Reports

The Week in Review

WEEK THIRTY-SIX

*Come and see what our God has done,
what awesome miracles he performs for people!*

Psalm 66:5 (NLT)

This Week's Prayer List
Week Thirty-Seven

I urge you, first of all, to pray for all people. Ask God to help them; intercede on their behalf, and give thanks for them.

1 Timothy 2:1 (NLT)

Name: _____

Date: _____

Prayer Request:
_____
_____
_____
_____

Name: _____

Date: _____

Prayer Request:
_____
_____
_____
_____

My Personal Prayer Requests
Week Thirty-Seven

Delight yourself also in the Lord, and He shall give you the desires of your heart. Commit your way to the Lord, trust also in Him, and He shall bring it to pass.

Psalm 37:4–5 (NKJV)

Date: _____

Prayer Request:

_____
_____
_____
_____
_____
_____
_____
_____

Scripture Promise:

_____
_____
_____

Quiet Moments with You
Daily Devotions

WEEK THIRTY-SEVEN

Then the Lord came and stood and called as at other times, "Samuel! Samuel!" And Samuel answered, "Speak, for Your servant hears."

1 Samuel 3:10 (**NKJV**)

MONDAY:

Date:

TUESDAY:

Date:

WEDNESDAY:

Date:

Speak to My Heart, Lord

THURSDAY:

Date:

FRIDAY:

Date:

SATURDAY:

Date:

Sunday Service

A Light for My Path

WEEK THIRTY-SEVEN

*I was glad when they said to me,
"Let us go into the house of the Lord."*

Psalm 122:1 (**NKJV**)

Date: _____ Speaker: _____

Sermon Title: _____

Scripture Text: _____

Notes:

_____
_____
_____
_____
_____
_____
_____
_____
_____
_____
_____
_____

Praise Reports

The Week in Review

WEEK THIRTY-SEVEN

*Come and see what our God has done,
what awesome miracles he performs for people!*

Psalm 66:5 (NLT)

This Week's Prayer List
Week Thirty-Eight

I urge you, first of all, to pray for all people. Ask God to help them; intercede on their behalf, and give thanks for them.

1 Timothy 2:1 (NLT)

Name: _____

Date: _____

Prayer Request:
_____
_____
_____
_____

Name: _____

Date: _____

Prayer Request:
_____
_____
_____
_____

My Personal Prayer Requests
Week Thirty-Eight

Delight yourself also in the Lord, and He shall give you the desires of your heart. Commit your way to the Lord, trust also in Him, and He shall bring it to pass.

Psalm 37:4–5 (NKJV)

Date: _____

Prayer Request:

Scripture Promise:

Quiet Moments with You
Daily Devotions

WEEK THIRTY-EIGHT

*Then the Lord came and stood and called as at other times,
"Samuel! Samuel!" And Samuel answered,
"Speak, for Your servant hears."*

1 Samuel 3:10 (NKJV)

MONDAY:

Date:

_____
_____
_____
_____
_____
_____
_____
_____
_____
_____
_____
_____
_____

TUESDAY:

Date:

WEDNESDAY:

Date:

Speak to My Heart, Lord

THURSDAY:

Date:

FRIDAY:

Date:

SATURDAY:

Date:

Sunday Service
A Light for My Path

WEEK THIRTY-EIGHT

I was glad when they said to me,
"Let us go into the house of the Lord."

Psalm 122:1 (**NKJV**)

Date: _____ Speaker: _____

Sermon Title: _____

Scripture Text: _____

Notes:

_____
_____
_____
_____
_____
_____
_____
_____
_____
_____

Praise Reports

The Week in Review

WEEK THIRTY-EIGHT

*Come and see what our God has done,
what awesome miracles he performs for people!*

Psalm 66:5 (**NLT**)

This Week's Prayer List

Week Thirty-Nine

I urge you, first of all, to pray for all people. Ask God to help them; intercede on their behalf, and give thanks for them.

1 Timothy 2:1 (NLT)

Name: _____

Date: _____

Prayer Request:
_____
_____
_____
_____

Name: _____

Date: _____

Prayer Request:
_____
_____
_____
_____

My Personal Prayer Requests
Week Thirty-Nine

Delight yourself also in the Lord, and He shall give you the desires of your heart. Commit your way to the Lord, trust also in Him, and He shall bring it to pass.

Psalm 37:4–5 (**NKJV**)

Date: _____

Prayer Request:

_____
_____
_____
_____
_____
_____
_____
_____

Scripture Promise:

_____
_____
_____

Quiet Moments with You
Daily Devotions

WEEK THIRTY-NINE

*Then the Lord came and stood and called as at other times,
"Samuel! Samuel!" And Samuel answered,
"Speak, for Your servant hears."*

1 Samuel 3:10 (**NKJV**)

MONDAY:

Date:

TUESDAY:

Date:

WEDNESDAY:

Date:

Speak to My Heart, Lord

THURSDAY:

Date:

FRIDAY:

Date:

SATURDAY:

Date:

Sunday Service
A Light for My Path

WEEK THIRTY-NINE

I was glad when they said to me,
"Let us go into the house of the Lord."

Psalm 122:1 (**NKJV**)

Date: _____ Speaker: _____

Sermon Title: _____

Scripture Text: _____

Notes:

_____
_____
_____
_____
_____
_____
_____
_____
_____
_____
_____
_____
_____

Praise Reports

The Week in Review

WEEK THIRTY-NINE

Come and see what our God has done,
what awesome miracles he performs for people!

Psalm 66:5 (NLT)

This Week's Prayer List
Week Forty

I urge you, first of all, to pray for all people. Ask God to help them; intercede on their behalf, and give thanks for them.

1 Timothy 2:1 (NLT)

Name: _____

Date: _____

Prayer Request:
_____
_____
_____
_____

Name: _____

Date: _____

Prayer Request:
_____
_____
_____
_____

My Personal Prayer Requests
Week Forty

Delight yourself also in the Lord, and He shall give you the desires of your heart. Commit your way to the Lord, trust also in Him, and He shall bring it to pass.

Psalm 37:4–5 (NKJV)

Date: _____

Prayer Request:

_____
_____
_____
_____
_____
_____
_____
_____
_____

Scripture Promise:

_____
_____
_____

Quiet Moments with You
Daily Devotions

WEEK FORTY

Then the Lord came and stood and called as at other times, "Samuel! Samuel!" And Samuel answered, "Speak, for Your servant hears."

1 Samuel 3:10 (**NKJV**)

MONDAY:

Date:

TUESDAY:

Date:

WEDNESDAY:

Date:

Speak to My Heart, Lord

THURSDAY:

Date:

FRIDAY:

Date:

SATURDAY:

Date:

Sunday Service

A Light for My Path

WEEK FORTY

*I was glad when they said to me,
"Let us go into the house of the Lord."*

Psalm 122:1 (NKJV)

Date: _____ Speaker: _____

Sermon Title: _____

Scripture Text: _____

Notes:

_____
_____
_____
_____
_____
_____
_____
_____
_____
_____

Praise Reports

The Week in Review

WEEK FORTY

*Come and see what our God has done,
what awesome miracles he performs for people!*

Psalm 66:5 (NLT)

This Week's Prayer List
Week Forty-One

I urge you, first of all, to pray for all people. Ask God to help them; intercede on their behalf, and give thanks for them.

1 Timothy 2:1 (NLT)

Name: _____

Date: _____

Prayer Request:

_____
_____
_____
_____

Name: _____

Date: _____

Prayer Request:

_____
_____
_____
_____

My Personal Prayer Requests
Week Forty-One

Delight yourself also in the Lord, and He shall give you the desires of your heart. Commit your way to the Lord, trust also in Him, and He shall bring it to pass.

Psalm 37:4–5 (NKJV)

Date: _____

Prayer Request:

_____
_____
_____
_____
_____
_____
_____
_____
_____
_____

Scripture Promise:

_____
_____
_____

Quiet Moments with You
Daily Devotions

WEEK FORTY-ONE

Then the Lord came and stood and called as at other times, "Samuel! Samuel!" And Samuel answered, "Speak, for Your servant hears."

1 Samuel 3:10 (NKJV)

MONDAY:

Date:

TUESDAY:

Date:

WEDNESDAY:

Date:

Speak to My Heart, Lord

THURSDAY:

Date:

FRIDAY:

Date:

SATURDAY:

Date:

Sunday Service
A Light for My Path

WEEK FORTY-ONE

*I was glad when they said to me,
"Let us go into the house of the Lord."*

Psalm 122:1 (**NKJV**)

Date: _____ Speaker: _____

Sermon Title: _____

Scripture Text: _____

Notes:

_____
_____
_____
_____
_____
_____
_____
_____
_____
_____
_____
_____

Praise Reports

The Week in Review

WEEK FORTY-ONE

*Come and see what our God has done,
what awesome miracles he performs for people!*

Psalm 66:5 (NLT)

This Week's Prayer List
Week Forty-Two

I urge you, first of all, to pray for all people. Ask God to help them; intercede on their behalf, and give thanks for them.

1 Timothy 2:1 (NLT)

Name: _____

Date: _____

Prayer Request:
_____
_____
_____
_____

Name: _____

Date: _____

Prayer Request:
_____
_____
_____
_____

My Personal Prayer Requests
Week Forty-Two

Delight yourself also in the Lord, and He shall give you the desires of your heart. Commit your way to the Lord, trust also in Him, and He shall bring it to pass.

Psalm 37:4–5 (**NKJV**)

Date: _____

Prayer Request:

Scripture Promise:

Quiet Moments with You
Daily Devotions

WEEK FORTY-TWO

Then the Lord came and stood and called as at other times, "Samuel! Samuel!" And Samuel answered, "Speak, for Your servant hears."

1 Samuel 3:10 (NKJV)

MONDAY:

Date:

TUESDAY:

Date:

WEDNESDAY:

Date:

Speak to My Heart, Lord

THURSDAY:

Date:

FRIDAY:

Date:

SATURDAY:

Date:

Sunday Service
A Light for My Path

WEEK FORTY-TWO

*I was glad when they said to me,
"Let us go into the house of the Lord."*

Psalm 122:1 (**NKJV**)

Date: _____ Speaker: _____

Sermon Title: _____

Scripture Text: _____

Notes:

_____
_____
_____
_____
_____
_____
_____
_____
_____
_____

EVERY DAY WITH YOU, LORD

Praise Reports

The Week in Review

WEEK FORTY-TWO

*Come and see what our God has done,
what awesome miracles he performs for people!*

Psalm 66:5 (NLT)

This Week's Prayer List
Week Forty-Three

I urge you, first of all, to pray for all people. Ask God to help them; intercede on their behalf, and give thanks for them.

1 Timothy 2:1 (NLT)

Name: _____

Date: _____

Prayer Request:

_____
_____
_____
_____

Name: _____

Date: _____

Prayer Request:

_____
_____
_____
_____

My Personal Prayer Requests
Week Forty-Three

Delight yourself also in the Lord, and He shall give you the desires of your heart. Commit your way to the Lord, trust also in Him, and He shall bring it to pass.

Psalm 37:4–5 (NKJV)

Date: _____

Prayer Request:

_____
_____
_____
_____
_____
_____
_____
_____

Scripture Promise:

_____
_____
_____

Quiet Moments with You
Daily Devotions

WEEK FORTY-THREE

*Then the Lord came and stood and called as at other times,
"Samuel! Samuel!" And Samuel answered,
"Speak, for Your servant hears."*

1 Samuel 3:10 (**NKJV**)

MONDAY:

Date:

TUESDAY:

Date:

WEDNESDAY:

Date:

Speak to My Heart, Lord

WEEK FORTY-THREE

THURSDAY:

Date:

FRIDAY:

Date:

SATURDAY:

Date:

Sunday Service

A Light for My Path

WEEK FORTY-THREE

I was glad when they said to me,
"Let us go into the house of the Lord."

Psalm 122:1 (**NKJV**)

Date: _____ Speaker: _____

Sermon Title: _____

Scripture Text: _____

Notes:

_____
_____
_____
_____
_____
_____
_____
_____
_____
_____
_____
_____

Praise Reports

The Week in Review

WEEK FORTY-THREE

Come and see what our God has done, what awesome miracles he performs for people!

Psalm 66:5 (NLT)

This Week's Prayer List
Week Forty-Four

I urge you, first of all, to pray for all people. Ask God to help them; intercede on their behalf, and give thanks for them.

1 Timothy 2:1 (NLT)

Name: _____

Date: _____

Prayer Request:
_____
_____
_____
_____

Name: _____

Date: _____

Prayer Request:
_____
_____
_____
_____

WEEK FORTY-FOUR

My Personal Prayer Requests
Week Forty-Four

Delight yourself also in the Lord, and He shall give you the desires of your heart. Commit your way to the Lord, trust also in Him, and He shall bring it to pass.

Psalm 37:4–5 (NKJV)

Date: _____

Prayer Request:

_____
_____
_____
_____
_____
_____
_____
_____

Scripture Promise:

_____
_____
_____

Quiet Moments with You
Daily Devotions

WEEK FORTY-FOUR

Then the Lord came and stood and called as at other times, "Samuel! Samuel!" And Samuel answered, "Speak, for Your servant hears."

1 Samuel 3:10 (**NKJV**)

MONDAY:

Date:

TUESDAY:

Date:

WEDNESDAY:

Date:

Speak to My Heart, Lord

THURSDAY:

Date:

FRIDAY:

Date:

SATURDAY:

Date:

Sunday Service

A Light for My Path

WEEK FORTY-FOUR

*I was glad when they said to me,
"Let us go into the house of the Lord."*

Psalm 122:1 (**NKJV**)

Date: _____ Speaker: _____

Sermon Title: _____

Scripture Text: _____

Notes:

_____
_____
_____
_____
_____
_____
_____
_____
_____
_____
_____
_____

Praise Reports

The Week in Review

WEEK FORTY-FOUR

*Come and see what our God has done,
what awesome miracles he performs for people!*

Psalm 66:5 (**NLT**)

This Week's Prayer List
Week Forty-Five

I urge you, first of all, to pray for all people. Ask God to help them; intercede on their behalf, and give thanks for them.

1 Timothy 2:1 (NLT)

Name: _____

Date: _____

Prayer Request:

_____
_____
_____
_____

Name: _____

Date: _____

Prayer Request:

_____
_____
_____
_____

My Personal Prayer Requests
Week Forty-Five

Delight yourself also in the Lord, and He shall give you the desires of your heart. Commit your way to the Lord, trust also in Him, and He shall bring it to pass.

Psalm 37:4–5 (**NKJV**)

Date: _____

Prayer Request:

_____
_____
_____
_____
_____
_____
_____
_____

Scripture Promise:

_____
_____
_____

Quiet Moments with You
Daily Devotions

WEEK FORTY-FIVE

*Then the Lord came and stood and called as at other times,
"Samuel! Samuel!" And Samuel answered,
"Speak, for Your servant hears."*

1 Samuel 3:10 (**NKJV**)

MONDAY:

Date:

TUESDAY:

Date:

WEDNESDAY:

Date:

Speak to My Heart, Lord

THURSDAY:

Date:

FRIDAY:

Date:

SATURDAY:

Date:

Sunday Service
A Light for My Path

WEEK FORTY-FIVE

I was glad when they said to me,
"Let us go into the house of the Lord."

Psalm 122:1 (**NKJV**)

Date: _____ Speaker: _____

Sermon Title: _____

Scripture Text: _____

Notes:

_____
_____
_____
_____
_____
_____
_____
_____
_____
_____

Praise Reports

The Week in Review

WEEK FORTY-FIVE

Come and see what our God has done,
what awesome miracles he performs for people!

Psalm 66:5 (NLT)

This Week's Prayer List
Week Forty-Six

I urge you, first of all, to pray for all people. Ask God to help them; intercede on their behalf, and give thanks for them.

1 Timothy 2:1 (NLT)

Name: _____

Date: _____

Prayer Request:

_____
_____
_____
_____

Name: _____

Date: _____

Prayer Request:

_____
_____
_____
_____

My Personal Prayer Requests
Week Forty-Six

Delight yourself also in the Lord, and He shall give you the desires of your heart. Commit your way to the Lord, trust also in Him, and He shall bring it to pass.

Psalm 37:4–5 (**NKJV**)

Date: _____

Prayer Request:

_____
_____
_____
_____
_____
_____
_____
_____
_____

Scripture Promise:

_____
_____
_____

Quiet Moments with You
Daily Devotions

WEEK FORTY-SIX

Then the Lord came and stood and called as at other times, "Samuel! Samuel!" And Samuel answered, "Speak, for Your servant hears."

1 Samuel 3:10 (NKJV)

MONDAY:

Date:

TUESDAY:

Date:

WEDNESDAY:

Date:

Speak to My Heart, Lord

THURSDAY:

Date:

FRIDAY:

Date:

SATURDAY:

Date:

Sunday Service

A Light for My Path

WEEK FORTY-SIX

I was glad when they said to me,
"Let us go into the house of the Lord."

Psalm 122:1 (**NKJV**)

Date: _____ Speaker: _____

Sermon Title: _____

Scripture Text: _____

Notes:

_____
_____
_____
_____
_____
_____
_____
_____
_____
_____
_____

Praise Reports

The Week in Review

WEEK FORTY-SIX

Come and see what our God has done,
what awesome miracles he performs for people!

Psalm 66:5 (NLT)

This Week's Prayer List
Week Forty-Seven

I urge you, first of all, to pray for all people. Ask God to help them; intercede on their behalf, and give thanks for them.

1 Timothy 2:1 (**NLT**)

Name: _____

Date: _____

Prayer Request:

_____
_____
_____
_____

Name: _____

Date: _____

Prayer Request:

_____
_____
_____
_____

My Personal Prayer Requests
Week Forty-Seven

Delight yourself also in the Lord, and He shall give you the desires of your heart. Commit your way to the Lord, trust also in Him, and He shall bring it to pass.

Psalm 37:4–5 (NKJV)

Date: _____

Prayer Request:

_____
_____
_____
_____
_____
_____
_____
_____

Scripture Promise:

_____
_____
_____

Quiet Moments with You
Daily Devotions

WEEK FORTY-SEVEN

Then the Lord came and stood and called as at other times, "Samuel! Samuel!" And Samuel answered, "Speak, for Your servant hears."

1 Samuel 3:10 (NKJV)

MONDAY:

Date:

TUESDAY:

Date:

WEDNESDAY:

Date:

Speak to My Heart, Lord

THURSDAY:

Date:

FRIDAY:

Date:

SATURDAY:

Date:

Sunday Service
A Light for My Path

WEEK FORTY-SEVEN

I was glad when they said to me,
"Let us go into the house of the Lord."

Psalm 122:1 (**NKJV**)

Date: _____ Speaker: _____

Sermon Title: _____

Scripture Text: _____

Notes:

_____
_____
_____
_____
_____
_____
_____
_____
_____
_____
_____
_____

Praise Reports

The Week in Review

WEEK FORTY-SEVEN

*Come and see what our God has done,
what awesome miracles he performs for people!*

Psalm 66:5 (NLT)

This Week's Prayer List
Week Forty-Eight

I urge you, first of all, to pray for all people. Ask God to help them; intercede on their behalf, and give thanks for them.

1 Timothy 2:1 (**NLT**)

Name: _____

Date: _____

Prayer Request:
_____
_____
_____
_____

Name: _____

Date: _____

Prayer Request:
_____
_____
_____
_____

My Personal Prayer Requests
Week Forty-Eight

Delight yourself also in the Lord, and He shall give you the desires of your heart. Commit your way to the Lord, trust also in Him, and He shall bring it to pass.

Psalm 37:4–5 (**NKJV**)

Date: _____

Prayer Request:

_____
_____
_____
_____
_____
_____
_____
_____

Scripture Promise:

_____
_____
_____

Quiet Moments with You
Daily Devotions

WEEK FORTY-EIGHT

Then the Lord came and stood and called as at other times, "Samuel! Samuel!" And Samuel answered, "Speak, for Your servant hears."

1 Samuel 3:10 (NKJV)

MONDAY:

Date:

TUESDAY:

Date:

WEDNESDAY:

Date:

Speak to My Heart, Lord

THURSDAY:

Date:

FRIDAY:

Date:

SATURDAY:

Date:

Sunday Service

A Light for My Path

WEEK FORTY-EIGHT

I was glad when they said to me,
"Let us go into the house of the Lord."

Psalm 122:1 (**NKJV**)

Date: _____ Speaker: _____

Sermon Title: _____

Scripture Text: _____

Notes:

_____
_____
_____
_____
_____
_____
_____
_____
_____
_____

Praise Reports

The Week in Review

WEEK FORTY-EIGHT

Come and see what our God has done,
what awesome miracles he performs for people!

Psalm 66:5 (NLT)

This Week's Prayer List
Week Forty-Nine

I urge you, first of all, to pray for all people. Ask God to help them; intercede on their behalf, and give thanks for them.

1 Timothy 2:1 (NLT)

Name: _____

Date: _____

Prayer Request:
_____
_____
_____
_____

Name: _____

Date: _____

Prayer Request:
_____
_____
_____
_____

My Personal Prayer Requests
Week Forty-Nine

Delight yourself also in the Lord, and He shall give you the desires of your heart. Commit your way to the Lord, trust also in Him, and He shall bring it to pass.

Psalm 37:4–5 (**NKJV**)

Date: _____

Prayer Request:

_____
_____
_____
_____
_____
_____
_____
_____

Scripture Promise:

_____
_____
_____

Quiet Moments with You
Daily Devotions

WEEK FORTY-NINE

Then the Lord came and stood and called as at other times, "Samuel! Samuel!" And Samuel answered, "Speak, for Your servant hears."

1 Samuel 3:10 (NKJV)

MONDAY:

Date:

TUESDAY:

Date:

WEDNESDAY:

Date:

Speak to My Heart, Lord

THURSDAY:

Date:

FRIDAY:

Date:

SATURDAY:

Date:

Sunday Service
A Light for My Path

WEEK FORTY-NINE

I was glad when they said to me,
"Let us go into the house of the Lord."

Psalm 122:1 (NKJV)

Date: _____ Speaker: _____

Sermon Title: _____

Scripture Text: _____

Notes:

_____
_____
_____
_____
_____
_____
_____
_____
_____
_____
_____

Praise Reports

The Week in Review

WEEK FORTY-NINE

*Come and see what our God has done,
what awesome miracles he performs for people!*

Psalm 66:5 (NLT)

This Week's Prayer List
Week Fifty

I urge you, first of all, to pray for all people. Ask God to help them; intercede on their behalf, and give thanks for them.

1 Timothy 2:1 (NLT)

Name: _____

Date: _____

Prayer Request:
_____
_____
_____
_____

Name: _____

Date: _____

Prayer Request:
_____
_____
_____
_____

My Personal Prayer Requests
Week Fifty

Delight yourself also in the Lord, and He shall give you the desires of your heart. Commit your way to the Lord, trust also in Him, and He shall bring it to pass.

Psalm 37:4–5 (NKJV)

Date: _____

Prayer Request:

_____
_____
_____
_____
_____
_____
_____
_____

Scripture Promise:

_____
_____
_____

Quiet Moments with You
Daily Devotions

WEEK FIFTY

*Then the Lord came and stood and called as at other times,
"Samuel! Samuel!" And Samuel answered,
"Speak, for Your servant hears."*

1 Samuel 3:10 (NKJV)

MONDAY:

Date:

TUESDAY:

Date:

WEDNESDAY:

Date:

Speak to My Heart, Lord

THURSDAY:

Date:

FRIDAY:

Date:

SATURDAY:

Date:

Sunday Service

A Light for My Path

WEEK FIFTY

I was glad when they said to me,
"Let us go into the house of the Lord."

Psalm 122:1 (**NKJV**)

Date: _____ Speaker: _____

Sermon Title: _____

Scripture Text: _____

Notes:

_____
_____
_____
_____
_____
_____
_____
_____
_____
_____

Praise Reports

The Week in Review

WEEK FIFTY

*Come and see what our God has done,
what awesome miracles he performs for people!*

Psalm 66:5 (NLT)

This Week's Prayer List

Week Fifty-One

I urge you, first of all, to pray for all people. Ask God to help them; intercede on their behalf, and give thanks for them.

1 Timothy 2:1 (NLT)

Name: _____

Date: _____

Prayer Request:

_____
_____
_____
_____

Name: _____

Date: _____

Prayer Request:

_____
_____
_____
_____

My Personal Prayer Requests
Week Fifty-One

Delight yourself also in the Lord, and He shall give you the desires of your heart. Commit your way to the Lord, trust also in Him, and He shall bring it to pass.

Psalm 37:4–5 (NKJV)

Date: _____

Prayer Request:

_____
_____
_____
_____
_____
_____
_____
_____
_____

Scripture Promise:

_____
_____
_____

Quiet Moments with You
Daily Devotions

WEEK FIFTY-ONE

Then the Lord came and stood and called as at other times, "Samuel! Samuel!" And Samuel answered, "Speak, for Your servant hears."

1 Samuel 3:10 (**NKJV**)

MONDAY:

Date:

TUESDAY:

Date:

WEDNESDAY:

Date:

Speak to My Heart, Lord

THURSDAY:

Date:

FRIDAY:

Date:

SATURDAY:

Date:

Sunday Service
A Light for My Path

WEEK FIFTY-ONE

I was glad when they said to me,
"Let us go into the house of the Lord."

Psalm 122:1 (**NKJV**)

Date: _____ Speaker: _____

Sermon Title: _____

Scripture Text: _____

Notes:

Praise Reports

The Week in Review

WEEK FIFTY-ONE

*Come and see what our God has done,
what awesome miracles he performs for people!*

Psalm 66:5 (NLT)

This Week's Prayer List
Week Fifty-Two

I urge you, first of all, to pray for all people. Ask God to help them; intercede on their behalf, and give thanks for them.

1 Timothy 2:1 (NLT)

Name: _____

Date: _____

Prayer Request:
_____
_____
_____
_____

Name: _____

Date: _____

Prayer Request:
_____
_____
_____
_____

My Personal Prayer Requests
Week Fifty-Two

Delight yourself also in the Lord, and He shall give you the desires of your heart. Commit your way to the Lord, trust also in Him, and He shall bring it to pass.

Psalm 37:4–5 (NKJV)

Date: _____

Prayer Request:

_____
_____
_____
_____
_____
_____
_____
_____
_____

Scripture Promise:

_____
_____
_____

Quiet Moments with You
Daily Devotions

WEEK FIFTY-TWO

Then the Lord came and stood and called as at other times, "Samuel! Samuel!" And Samuel answered, "Speak, for Your servant hears."

1 Samuel 3:10 (**NKJV**)

MONDAY:

Date:

TUESDAY:

Date:

WEDNESDAY:

Date:

Speak to My Heart, Lord

THURSDAY:

Date:

FRIDAY:

Date:

SATURDAY:

Date:

Sunday Service
A Light for My Path

WEEK FIFTY-TWO

I was glad when they said to me,
"Let us go into the house of the Lord."

Psalm 122:1 (**NKJV**)

Date: _____ Speaker: _____

Sermon Title: _____

Scripture Text: _____

Notes:

_____
_____
_____
_____
_____
_____
_____
_____
_____
_____
_____
_____

# Praise Reports

The Week in Review

WEEK FIFTY-TWO

*Come and see what our God has done,
what awesome miracles he performs for people!*

Psalm 66:5 (NLT)

THE FAITHFULNESS OF GOD REVEALED
The Year in Review

How the king rejoices in your strength, O LORD! He shouts with joy because you give him victory. For you have given him his heart's desire; you have withheld nothing he requested.

Psalm 21:1–2 (NLT)

Well, by now you have recorded an entire year of prayer requests, both those prayed for yourself as well as for others. You have spent daily devotional time with God and taken notes from the preaching of the Word of God delivered from the pulpit each Sunday morning. All these things taken together when pondered, can be an ever-ready reminder of God's love, care, and individual concern for you. As you look back over what you have written and review your daily entries and the words spoken to you directly from the Father's heart, you will begin to see a pattern of God's faithfulness to you in the answers to prayer, and in His ever-constant presence in your life.

Many times throughout the Book of Psalms we see the word *Selah*, which means to pause and calmly think of what has just been spoken. Contained within this journal, is your very own personal record of quiet moments spent with your God and Father over the past year. These can help you to see, more clearly than ever before, His loving kindness expressly for you. As you review each page, you will see *The Faithfulness of God Revealed*.

It should both comfort you as well as inspire and build up your faith as you look back on the prayers you prayed and how the Lord answered them, worked things out, and, as a gentle Shepherd, faithfully brought you through.

The word faithful is defined as, *steady in allegiance or affection; loyal; constant, reliable, trusted; faithful assurances of help*.[2] The word trusted, surfaces once again. Do you remember beginning the year with the definition of the word trust? We found its meaning to be, *reliance on the integrity, strength or ability of a person or thing; confident expectation of something; hope; one upon which a person relies*.[3]

We have trusted in the strength, integrity, and ability of our God all through the year. As we come to its close, we have found that the Lord is absolutely faithful and can indeed be confidently relied upon to keep His promises, walk with, and yes, even *carry* us when necessary, as we fulfill His destiny, purpose and plans for our lives.

Looking forward to a new year ahead, we can stand with our feet planted firmly on the Rock of our salvation, Christ Jesus our Lord. We can, as did Father Abraham, be unwavering and confident in knowing that He *is* faithful who promised to never leave us or forsake us, and to be our ever-present help in every facet of our lives. Whatever the request, be it for self, family, friend or foe, there is nothing too hard for the Lord to handle. AMEN!

---

[2] *Webster's Universal College Dictionary* (2001), s.v. "faithful."
[3] *Webster's Universal College Dictionary* (2001), s.v. "trust."

My Song of Gratitude

*Oh, sing to the L*ORD *a new song! for He has done marvellous things; His right hand and His holy arm have gained Him the victory.*

Psalm 98:1 (NKJV)

GREAT IS THY FAITHFULNESS

Thomas O. Chisholm, William M. Runyan
Copyright 1923. Renewal 1951 Hope Publishing Co. Carol Stream, IL. 60187.
Public Domain.

Great is Thy faithfulness, O God my Father,
there is no shadow of turning with Thee;
Thou changest not, Thy compassions, they fail not,
as Thou hast been, Thou forever wilt be.

Great is Thy faithfulness! Great is Thy faithfulness!
Morning by morning new mercies I see;
all I have needed Thy hand hath provided.
Great is Thy faithfulness, Lord unto me!

Summer and winter, and springtime and harvest,
sun, moon and stars in their courses above,
Join with all nature in manifold witness,
to Thy great faithfulness, mercy and love.

Great is Thy faithfulness! Great is Thy faithfulness!
Morning by morning new mercies I see;
all I have needed Thy hand hath provided.
Great is Thy faithfulness, Lord unto me!

Pardon for sin and a peace that endureth,
Thine own dear presence to cheer and to guide,
Strength for today and bright hope for tomorrow,
blessings all mine, with ten thousand beside!

Great is Thy faithfulness! Great is Thy faithfulness!
Morning by morning new mercies I see;
all I have needed Thy hand hath provided.
Great is Thy faithfulness, Lord unto me!

Daily inspiration from God's Word to build your faith, overcome discouragement, and experience hope. Look for it soon to begin your journey and let **Hope Arise**!

www.ingramcontent.com/pod-product-compliance
Lightning Source LLC
Chambersburg PA
CBHW060558170426
43201CB00009B/824